One's past is what one is.
The only way by which people should be judged.
— Oscar Wilde

Preface: You have a book inside you

For years, my mom has said that I have a book inside me. Maybe that's the reason for my longstanding GERD.

I started a blog, "Marianne's Musings," a couple of years before I retired from my full-time communications job with American Red Cross Blood Services. The week after I concluded nearly 34 years of service with the Red Cross, I started freelancing for **Our Town**, a local weekly published by Schurz Publications.

I cover several local non-profits, including writing a series of "On the Job in Our Town" features for which I volunteer behind the scenes to provide a unique look at each agency's work.

Each month, I also write two or three columns in which I often share a humorous slice-of-life experience. When I worked at the Red Cross, people would sometimes tell me they saw me on television. When I started freelancing for **Our Town,** people said they particularly enjoyed my columns (above which appeared my photo) about Galla, my rescue dog, and my relationship with my mom.

Two and a half years later, after I started a column with one of my mom's sayings ("pick up after yourself and put things back where you found them,") the idea for "the book I had inside me" came to me.

I would attempt to write about all the things my mother taught me, using a dose of humor and plenty of heart.

~~~~~

Now, some family background.

I'm descended from at least three generations of strong, independent women on mom's side. Even though these independent-minded women married, they retained a fierce streak of knowing their own mind.

My memories begin with my maternal grandmother, Mary Mateljan Lugar. Barely five feet tall, my grandmother may have well been the inspiration for Shakespeare's oft-quoted line from **A Midsummer's Night Dream** if the bard had lived in the early 20th century.

"Though she be but little, she is fierce!"

Grandma Mary was born in the Cambria City section of my hometown of Johnstown, Pennsylvania, in December of 1903. (Cambria City was named after the Cambria Iron Works that employed thousands.) She was the second of four children. When grandma was a toddler, her mother was diagnosed with tuberculosis. Not wanting her offspring to grow up lacking maternal affection, great-grandma insisted that the family return to present-day Croatia, where the grandparents resided. Great-grandma Mateljan died when grandma was 5.

Although she loved her grandparents, Grandma Mary longed to return to the small western Pennsylvania town where she was born. She did several odd jobs, including carrying water for households in the village. She saved the money earned from such work, and when she saved enough for a rosary, she asked her grandmother to buy her one. She prayed her rosary, asking God to return home. She was finally able to do so after World War I.

My great-grandfather Mateljan, who traveled back and forth to the United States, provided grandma financial assistance to return to America. At age 17, she boarded the ship and crossed the Atlantic – all by herself. Great-grandfather met her in New York, and when he asked her where she wanted to go, she replied she wanted to return to the house where she was born.

Back in Johnstown, grandma did housework and worked as a dishwasher at the long-gone Capital Hotel. The head cook, seeing that grandma was a diligent worker, chose her to be his helper.

She met and married my grandfather, Joseph, and they raised six children. She managed the family purse strings, just as my mom would later do.

Grandpa Lugar worked in his family's butcher shop, also in Cambria City. Great-grandfather Lugar died when grandpa was 12; a couple of years later great-grandmother Lugar asked their priest to fudge grandpa's age on a new baptismal certificate so grandpa could get a job at Bethlehem Steel. He worked in the Machine Shop of the Cambria Iron Works for more than 50 years. His mother died when he was 17.

Grandpa Lugar was so skilled in woodworking and repairs that after my grandparents bought a house of their own, he removed and reversed three flights of stairs, plus completed additional renovations each year. In what spare time he had, Grandpa Lugar enjoyed music, particularly the opera, photography and the movies.

My grandparents' first child, my Uncle Joe, was diagnosed with polio as an infant. Lest you think that only female members of the Mateljan-Lugar family were strong-willed, I will note that Uncle Joe learned to walk on crutches and did so for 85 years until a year or so before his death at age 91.

Since Uncle Joe was unable to work in Bethlehem Steel, long the main employer in Johnstown, my grandparents scrimped so he could attend a local business college. He also learned photography. For years, he worked in the business office of a local coal mine during the week and took wedding pictures on Saturdays. He also handcrafted knotty pine cabinets and created hand-welded wrought iron chairs for the kitchen in the home where he and my Aunt Naomi raised their three children.

~~~~~

My mom, Betty, was the fourth child and second daughter. She struggled in school, partly because of her eyesight, and especially had trouble spelling. Mom left high school after her sophomore year to work in a sewing factory.

Some would say my mom isn't smart. I would caution those of that belief not to confuse education with intelligence. My mom is one of the wisest people I know. She enjoys word puzzles, reading the newspaper and non-fiction books. Thanks to Grandpa Lugar's genes, my mom can figure things out. She, not my dad, led them in laying linoleum in their bathroom. She figured out how to fit second-hand cabinets in a corner of our kitchen ahead of a family friend who built his family's home. She could get to the bottom of many problems that my dad couldn't.

My parents married relatively late by 1950s standards. She was nearly 27, and he had just turned 25. She had trouble conceiving and had a procedure done to enable pregnancy. Born on Sept. 15, the Memorial of Our Lady of Sorrows, mom prayed to the Blessed Virgin Mary to get pregnant, promising that if she had a daughter, she would be named for her and her mother, Anne.

I came along on Oct. 7, the Feast of Our Lady of the Rosary, when dad was 27 and mom had just turned 29. True to mom's word, I was named Marianne – not Mary Ann – so my name would not be shortened.

Over the years, I've shocked many when I've noted that I know of at least one other "Marianne Spampinato." They respond that it can't be. I then tell them about my dad's brother, Jim, who relocated to Michigan, where he met and married a woman of French Canadian descent named Marianne.

~~~~~

I was an unintentional only child. My mom was the disciplinarian when I was growing up, not my dad. I don't recall ever hearing the situation comedy cliché, "Wait until your father gets home!" When I misbehaved, mom administered the spanking or sent me to my room.

Not long after we moved into the house my parents purchased in 1964, months before I started kindergarten, mom underwent breast surgery, which, fortunately, did not result in a cancer diagnosis. She was stressed, just the same.

While mom was in the hospital, I stayed with my parents' former landlords, who spoiled me rotten.

When I returned home after mom was released from the hospital, I balked at her direction and refused to obey. When she insisted, I had a temper tantrum and cried that I was going to run away from home.

Mom, calling my bluff, told me to go ahead and leave. Having no fallback position, I sniffed and exited the front door and sat on the porch and cried. Mom told me to get off the porch.

Where could I go? I didn't have a way to my grandparents or the couple I had stayed with while mom was in the hospital. I went to the side of the house, still sobbing.

After a while, she asked me if I was going to listen and obey, and I said that I would. She let me re-enter our house.

When my dad came home from work, he was aghast that mom let me leave. Years later, mom admitted that if I had indeed taken a hike, she would have had to come after me.

Lord only knows how I would have behaved in the years to follow had I gotten one over mom on this one. This incident wasn't the last argument between mom and me, but it was the last time I threatened to leave home.

I share this experience because many people assume that every only child is spoiled rotten. That certainly was not the case in the home where I grew up, at least in the eyes of a neighbor whose daughter I played with and fellow parishioners who asked my parents which one disciplined me.

~~~~~

For my fellow baby boomers, my mom's words of wisdom may remind them of guidance from their own parents. If so, then I hope this book brings back memories of loved ones and bygone times. Maybe my anecdotes will make you chuckle.

As Epictetus said, "He who laughs at himself never runs out of things to laugh at."

Much more recently, Ted, a former work supervisor, said, "If you can laugh at it, you can live with it."

Although I've never had children, I find I sound like my mom when correcting my rescue dog, Galla. (See "Don't eat that…you don't know where it's been" and "Watch where you're going and look both ways before you cross the street.")

As for those years away from AARP membership, well, I hope you will appreciate my mom's wisdom, take it to heart – and pass it on.

Marianne
Spampinato,
December 2017

Table of Contents

Just DON'T do it

Don't wear white shoes before
Memorial Day or after Labor Day .... Page 16
Don't play with your food (clean your plate) .... Page 18
Don't eat that…you don't know where it's been .... Page 23
Don't snack between meals................................. Page 24
Don't let the bedbugs bite................................. Page 25
Don't turn your feet, you'll stretch your shoes .... Page 27
Don't rush – take your time................................ Page 28
Don't talk to or take rides with strangers .... Page 31
Don't touch that .... Page 36
Don't talk money, family business, politics or
religion with people you don't know well
(and mind your own business)............................ Page 39
Don't say "never" or "always"............................. Page 43
If your friends jumped in the lake, would you?............. Page 44
Don't suck your thumb................................... Page 46
Don't wish your life away................................. Page 48
Don't get a fat Christmas tree – but do use white lights..... Page 49

Please do…

Pick up after yourself and put things
back where you found them .... Page 56
You get what you pay for…and
take care of your investment .... Page 59
Chocolate makes your face break out.................... Page 62
Get plenty of rest.. Page 63
With your naturally curly hair, you should wear
your hair short... Page 64

Wear clean underwear – you never know when you'll be in an accident .... Page 69
Wear your Sunday best .... Page 74
Tell the truth…it's easier than trying to remember a lie .... Page 78
You're not going to work in a sewing factory .... Page 85
Say please and thank you .... Page 90
Be humble .... Page 92
Listen to your gut .... Page 94
Everything comes in threes .... Page 95
Take care of your teeth .... Page 96
Take care of your our back and stand up straight .... Page 97
Under, not over .... Page 99
Plain black (coffee) .... Page 100
Short takes: The fruit doesn't fall far from the tree; It could always be worse; Watch where you're going and look both ways before you cross the street; Be careful what you wish for...you might get it ... Page 101-102

A mother's faith and love

God writes straight with crooked lines .... Page 104
You never know what you can do until you try .... Page 106
Walk with God: When God closes a door, He opens a window .... Page 111
We pray in our time, but God answers in His time .... Page 112
Let me kiss it and make it better .... Page 115

Published by the Daily American

All rights reserved. No part of this work may be reproduced or used in any form or by any means, graphic, electronic or digital without written permission of the Daily American, 334 West Main St., Somerset, PA 15501, 814-444-5900, or the Author Marianne Spampinato.

Just Don't Do It

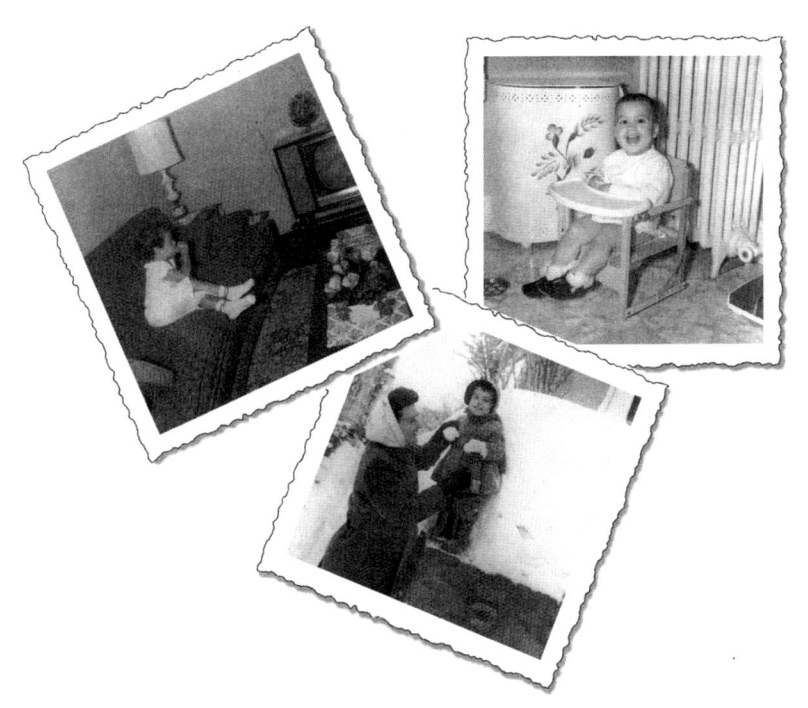

Don't wear white shoes before Memorial Day or after Labor Day

When I was a kid, at most we had four color choices for sneakers, or, as they were called back then, tennis shoes: white, red, dark blue, and black. As for brands of tennis shoes, well, there were Keds. Keds were made from canvas and had laces – no zippers or Velcro closures.

And no, we didn't feel deprived. You don't miss what you never had.

The main problem with white Keds is that they easily became soiled. Some stains didn't completely come out in the wash. In such cases, out came the glass bottle of Hollywood Sani-White polish.

I can still picture the Sani-White cartons, which featured either a photo of a nurse wearing a nurse's cap or a photo of an infant (who presumably wears white baby shoes).

We'd shake the bottle, then take the small piece of stiff fabric packaged with the polish and apply Sani-White on our sneakers and dress shoes.

Well of course I wore white shoes when I made my First Communion.

You'd have to lay down a thick coat to cover scuffs, then wait for the polish to dry before buffing (sometimes, you'd see that a second coat of polish was needed) – fortunately, only dress shoes required buffing.

As for your newly polished white Keds, they left a trail of white dust wherever you went. More often than not, I would leave white scuff marks on our furniture. And I always had white feet when I took my shoes off.

Keeping my white shoes looking immaculate seemed a never-ending task to a kid with big feet who seemed to get her white shoes dirty minutes after they were polished. When I was a teen, I heard that nail polish remover could remove scuffs. However, if you rubbed the scuff too hard, the shoe's finish also wore off.

It's no wonder that I came to detest white shoes, and stopped wearing them before, during and after Labor Day.

Don't play with your food (clean your plate)

One of my favorite photos from childhood is one in which I'm seated in my high chair eating buttered macaroni. Look at the photo for as long as you want, but you won't see a plate, fork, spoon or napkin. Just my greasy little hands, pushing my food around and picking it up from the tray of my high chair.

Nearly six decades later, I'm still amazed that mom let me eat like this. After all, my parents taught me to eat properly, to use a knife, fork and spoon – and chew with my mouth closed. And mom counted on me to set the table when we had company for dinner.

Our meals were probably like those in many Caucasian-owned homes in small town America during the second half of the 20th century: fried chicken, breaded pork chops, Swiss steak, beef roast, pork roast, spaghetti and pancakes; then a baked ham, stuffed chicken or turkey on holidays. Almost all meat entrees were served with mashed potatoes and gravy. Never rice, occasionally sweet potatoes or what we called "onion potatoes" – boiled cubed potatoes added to butter and sautéed onions.

Mom recalls my being a somewhat picky eater. I didn't like meat loaf, stuffed peppers, chili (kidney beans – ugh!), even though mom made them often because dad loved such fare. I also wasn't crazy about most vegetables. So, I often dawdled in cleaning my plate when we had such fare for supper.

Never met a kid who doesn't like peanut butter and jelly sandwiches? Well, you haven't met me. Sure, I spread jelly, jam or preserves on toast and English muffins. I'll eat peanut butter crackers and fudge. But the two of them together? No way!

Usually once a week (Tuesdays, if I recall correctly), the parochial school I attended from grades three through eight served chicken rice soup and peanut butter and jelly sandwiches in the cafeteria for lunch. So, on those days, I had nothing to eat but a small bowl of chicken rice soup between breakfast and supper.

Trust me, you wouldn't have believed that I was such a picky eater if you saw a photo of me during adolescence.

Even in recent years, whenever mom made her delicious beef vegetable soup, I avoid eating the lima beans. Recently, she started separating the soup into two pots and added lima beans only to the batch for her. And I still won't eat kidney beans. However, now when I cook for mom and me, I prepare fresh green beans, broccoli, cauliflower, carrots or asparagus (in season).

~~~~~

When I was a kid, eating out at McDonald's was a rare treat, even though hamburgers cost less than a quarter. We just didn't have the disposable income to "splurge" until mom had returned to work full-time when I was in elementary school.

I remember years ago when a former CEO and his wife moved to Johnstown, they were surprised that they could not order pirohy and other ethnic food in restaurants. I replied that when we went to a restaurant, we usually wanted to eat something that we wouldn't make at home, such as seafood or veal parmesan. I added that ethnic fare was a staple at local church festivals.

Over time, this changed as each successive generation descended from Eastern European immigrants prepared less ethnic fare at home. In mom's case, she roasted lamb and made halupki (pigs in the blanket) and haluski, but stopped making home-made pirohy decades ago, and never made a strudel. Too much work when she worked outside our home full-time. Instead she would make pan pirohy using lasagna noodles.

I watched my Grandma Lugar make apple strudel from scratch. She'd pull the dough so it was paper thin and covered her kitchen table. No pre-made phyllo dough. When she donated a strudel to a church bake sale, it was usually sold whole or in halves at a total cost of $24. A pan of my mom's peanut butter fudge, cut into 48 pieces, sold for the same amount (mom would be angry if her fudge was sold for more than 50 cents per piece). Not to diminish my mom's efforts and generosity, but we're talking a day's worth of work for my grandma versus about an hour or so of effort per pan by my mom.

My dad often looked forward to mom being laid off from the sewing factory so we would enjoy home-cooked meals, pies and cakes. I lived at home when I attended the University of Pittsburgh at Johnstown, obtaining a bachelor's degree in Journalism. My classes usually ended before my parents' work days, so I prepared supper. After I landed my 8 a.m. to 5 p.m. job at the American Red Cross, at which I usually put in more than 40 hours a week, dad's home-cooked meals ended, too, at least until mom retired.

My parents and I gradually broadened our dining experiences and came to savor Chinese food and barbecued spare ribs, which are difficult to eat without using your hands. Eat them with a knife and fork and you'll never clean the bones as generations of Lugar men and women have enjoyed doing. (My Aunt Donna and I had a double dose of the Lugar gene that made us crave the crispy roasted skin of a chicken or turkey. Before the meal was served, you'd find us standing over the bird, fighting over the roasted skin.)

I doubt few people could clean meat off bones more thoroughly or more quickly than my mom. If someone held a bone chewing contest on the Fourth of July, my money would be on my mom.

Years later, when my parents and I dined at Red Lobster, I'd often order a side of snow crab clusters. Now, that's really playing with one's food. Mom and dad couldn't understand why anyone would want to invest so much time for relatively little food.

Then one day when mom was in her mid-70s, I challenged her to "try it, you'll like it." She did. And she so enjoyed snow crab clusters that she often ordered a pound of them for her meal, not as a side, as I usually did.

Dad was a slow eater, while mom and I consumed our meal more quickly – too quickly, in dad's eyes. So, whenever mom and I had snow crab clusters (dad never indulged and ate crab only when it was formed into crab cakes), we'd all finish eating at the same time. Amen.

~~~~~

When it comes to Galla, the rescue dog, I want her to play with her food. She practically inhales food poured into a typical dog food bowl. A couple times, she ate so fast that she regurgitated her food, then ate what she regurgitated. Yuck!

I've purchased several "slow feed" bowls with labyrinth and puzzle patterns so Galla has to pick around obstacles to get at her food. So far, these bowls have successfully prevented regurgitation, so by all means, Galla, play with your food.

MOM'S PEANUT BUTTER FUDGE RECIPE

My mom received this recipe from the landlord of the apartment where we lived until I was nearly four. My mom has tweaked the recipe, as indicated by italicized text:

Two 1 lb. boxes of powdered sugar plus 6 heaping tablespoons of powdered sugar *(From my mom's experience, do not use powdered sugar sold in bags.)*
One can evaporated milk
One stick butter (1/4 pound)
One 28-ounce jar of creamy peanut butter
One 16-ounce container of *Fluff* marshmallow cream *(Trust mom; other brands don't work as well.)*

Cook until soft ball stage, stirring frequently. Then remove from heat and add peanut butter and marshmallow cream. Beat with electric mixer until creamy and think. Pour into buttered jelly roll pan (15.5" x 10.5" x 1"). Cool.

Yields six pounds of fudge, cut into 48 1" pieces.

Don't eat that…you don't know where it's been

If I wouldn't clean my plate during dinner, then I certainly was forbidden to eat anything from an unknown source.

And I was a kid long before the Tylenol tampering scandal.

We went trick-or-treating only to houses owned by people we knew. No piling into cars and driving to neighboring municipalities that held trick-or-treat night on different evenings than in our municipality. No eating candy or other treats unless they were in a sealed package.

Ever since I adopted Galla, I've channeled my mom most often with this command. When we take our daily walk, I must be on high alert for anything remotely edible that may tempt Galla. Such treats include, but are not limited to, slices of pizza; half-eaten hamburgers, hot dogs and breakfast sandwiches; and pieces of fruit. And then there are the occasional carcasses of birds, mice, chipmunks, squirrels, raccoons and groundhogs in various stages of decomposition.

Unfortunately, I have so far been unsuccessful in correcting her belief in the kibble fairy, a sprite that leaves kibble-sized treats in our yard. No matter how many times I've tried to tell her otherwise, she fails to understand that the rabbits in our suburban area are the actual source for her "treats."

Don't snack between meals

I've had a weight problem since I was in elementary school. And at least in my case, having a weight problem – along with wearing glasses and braces – made me more, not less, likely to eat between meals.

When I was in high school, I stopped snacking. No matter how many hunger pangs I had in the evening, I would not snack. Plus, I walked approximately two and a half miles each day to and from school.

By my senior year, I was at last within the recommended weight range for my height, but my significant weight loss affected by health. I lost so much weight that my menstrual cycle stopped temporarily.

During college, I gained the "freshman 15" and then some. My weight gain continued during my full-time career, although I would yoyo – lose a few pounds, then gain them back (and more, all too often).

Uninterested in maintaining a gym membership, I walked around town and side roads once the Red Cross relocated to the suburbs. Nowadays, Galla and I typically walk at least two miles each day, unless there's snow and ice on the ground, when we walk at least a mile. Several years ago, our family physician told me that he didn't care what I ate, as long as I moved. Walk, run, whatever, I need to move my body.

When I retired from the Red Cross, I set a goal of losing at least 30 pounds (and keeping them off). I dropped 12 pounds in the first year, then maintained for another year or so, then started losing weight again. As of this writing, about four pounds, but it's better than gaining four pounds.

Don't let the bedbugs bite

When I was a kid, at bedtime my parents would say, "Nighty night, sleep tight – and don't let the bedbugs bite."

Scary, right? Didn't my parents know that children need their sleep? It's a wonder I got any sleep. No wonder now when I see bugs, any kind of bugs, I feel itchy. I feel itchy even writing about them.

I hadn't thought of this nightly ritual for years until several years ago when the news media aired report after report of outbreaks of bedbugs in major cities in the United States and around the world.

During my tenure at the American Red Cross, I often traveled to special event blood drives and various meetings. Most travel consisted of day trips. However, each year I had a couple of trips requiring spending one or more nights in a hotel.

My mom, who watches entirely too much television news, became obsessed with news about the blood-sucking pests, and soon came to believe there were hordes of bedbugs hiding behind every hotel room door.

So, before I left on a trip, my mom would remind me to check my hotel room for bedbugs. Likewise, she warned me against putting my purse down on the floor of the local movie theater or most public places. You just never know.

When I had the opportunity to select my own hotel, I was sure to use bedbugregistry.com. Of course, there's such a website; now there's also bedbugreport.com. Such registries are free; users can search their databases of user-submitted bedbug reports from across the United States and in other countries.

I didn't just pay lip service to mom's advice. After all, she would be sure to ask me about it when I called to let my parents know that I had arrived safely. Honesty is the best policy (see chapter

"Tell the truth").

My diligence started by including a flashlight in my suitcase. When I entered the hotel room, I first headed to the bed. I pulled down the spread, moved the pillows, and picked up the mattress cover and checked for small specks of blood on and under the mattress and along the edge of the box springs. I checked the sheets and took the covers off a couple of pillows. I checked all around and behind the baseboard. I inspected the corners and other furniture in the room, including cushions of the couch and chairs.

Even though I never found any evidence of bedbugs, I played it safe by keeping my clothing in my luggage, not in dresser drawers. Sometimes, I even packed garbage bags and kept my luggage in them, just in case.

You bet I slept tight, well, as tight as you can in a strange room in noisy hotel, and the bed bugs didn't bite.

Don't turn your feet, you'll stretch your shoes

My dad wore size 13 shoes; mom wore size 9 to 10, preferably 9½ but as large half-sizes became difficult to find, settled in at size 10 wide. So, there was no way I was going end up a size 7.

I eventually grew into a size 10 wide. Plus, I have a flat left foot. Not long after I started to walk, my parents spared no expense to buy me special Stride Rite shoes to correct the arching in my left foot, to no avail. In time, as my feet grew and I needed new shoes every year, they admitted defeat and accepted the fact of my flat left foot.

I didn't help matters by occasionally twisting my foot on its side when I stood. Being somewhat shy, I think I did it out of nervousness. But when mom caught me, she reminded me to stop it so I wouldn't stretch my big shoes or affect my balance.

Don't rush – take your time

When I was young(er), I always seemed to be in hurry. Even one of the nominations for the American Red Cross Tiffany Award for Employee Excellence that I received early in my communications career included something about me rushing through the halls.

One Friday afternoon shortly before I bought my first home, I was (literally) running some errands in downtown Johnstown on my lunch break when I caught the heel of my shoe in one of my trouser cuffs and fell. This was before I started wearing sneakers while out on errands. I tore my pants, scuffed my knee and sprained my big left toe. It hurt like heck.

Mom had previously warned me about cuffed slacks, so I was hoping the pain would subside before I went home. Fat chance. Not only did the pain not decrease, it seemed to intensify throughout the afternoon.

After work, I limped over to the hospital emergency room about two blocks away from the Red Cross. They x-rayed my left foot and told me I had broken my big toe.

I was fitted for a pair of crutches and told to try to stay off my feet.

But wait, it gets worse. I was scheduled to leave the next morning for the Red Cross National Convention in San Diego. On an airplane. By myself. I was to arrive the day before other local delegates so I could set up an exhibit.

I can't remember (or don't want to remember) what mom said when I finally got home, but to say she wasn't pleased would be an understatement.

(At this point, I should add that of all the sewing mom has done for me over the years, hemming cuffed pants was her least favorite task. She urged me not to wear them, perhaps knowing I was an accident waiting to happen.)

Since I was to fly out of Johnstown, I had to be driven only to the local airport. I was surprised I was able to stretch my left leg on the commuter flight to Pittsburgh.

I had been assigned a window seat on the flight to San Diego. I approached the ticket counter, showed them the single crutch I had agreed to take along, explained about my left foot and asked to be moved to a "left-hanging" aisle seat so I could occasionally stretch my left leg.

When we boarded, I found that I had been moved to a "right-hanging" aisle seat. After everyone was seated, the flight attendants were able to move me to a left-hanging aisle seat.

After the flight landed, I headed for the baggage claim area, where I stayed well behind everyone else. Or so I thought. After two women in front of me retrieved all of their luggage, they picked up their bags, swung them backward, and one of them hit the knee I had fallen on. Owwww!

Somehow, I managed to put up our exhibit on my own, and took the doctor's advice and sat when I could. By the end of the convention, I could wear casual shoes comfortably.

~~~~~

My handwriting is so sloppy, I probably should have become a doctor. I start out neatly, but as my thoughts race, I write faster to keep up, and whatever I'm writing ends up a mess.

My mom has considered my penmanship atrocious for years. When she met with my third-grade teacher during the school's open house, mom asked her what she thought about my handwriting.

Sister hemmed and hawed and acknowledged that it could be

better. Mom urged my teacher to give me the grade I deserved in penmanship. I received a "C." Mom thought that was too generous a grade.

The "C" did nothing to motivate me to try harder. Cursed cursive writing!

Don't talk to or take rides with strangers

I was a kid when in a town the size of Johnstown it was generally safe to walk a mile or more in any direction. We played in our yards, in the alleys, and in our streets.

Just how safe was it? When I was a kid, I usually accompanied my mom downtown when she shopped at the (long-gone and much lamented) Penn Traffic department store.

Sometimes, though, mom was shopping for me, so she didn't want me to see what she was buying. She would take me to the mezzanine, where I would sit in one of the chairs and read a book. Before she went on her own for a half-hour or so, she would remind me, "Don't talk with strangers. Don't go anywhere with a stranger. Stay here and wait for me."

One of Grandma Lugar's cousins worked in the women's restroom near the mezzanine seating, so she was usually able to keep an eye on me.

My mom occasionally looks back on my childhood and regrets being overly protective of me.

But just think if our Penn Traffic routine happened in the present day. My mom could possibly be charged with child endangerment!

~~~~~

Because we lived more than four miles from the parochial school I attended from second through eighth grade, I took a bus that also picked up students from several local municipalities.

Interestingly, that bus line required riders to leave school a few minutes before other students. Sometimes when our teachers delayed our departure, we'd miss the bus. Apparently under no obligation to wait, the bus driver left without us.

No recrimination, no public outrage, no investigation followed. I just walked a couple of blocks to stay with my Grandparents Lugar until my parents picked me up.

After grade school, I attended Bishop McCort Catholic High School, which is located a little more than a mile from where I grew up.

Like other teens who lived the same distance from school, I walked to school. It took me 20 minutes most days, maybe five minutes longer in wintry weather. No matter the weather, the rule remained, "Don't ride with strangers. Don't talk with strangers."

Mom supports me in measuring that I was as tall as an early 1960s snowfall.

YES, THAT'S RIGHT, WE HAD SCHOOL WHEN IT SNOWED.

Nowadays, schools often cancel the night before a predicted snowfall, long before snowflakes fly.

Someday, when I'm in a nursing home and there's no one available to wipe the drool from my mouth (or from any other body part that needs wiping) because the younger generation is afraid to drive in the snow, I hope I still have my mind to be pissed. Really pissed.

~~~~~

One of my traits my dad was proudest of was my good sense of direction – as in finding my way around with or without use of a map. This was a LONG time before GPS.

With my good sense of direction, we had to ask for directions less often than other families when we went on vacation.

He never tired of telling a story from our first trip to Washington, D.C., when I was about 10 years old. One afternoon, we went to the Franciscan Monastery and wanted to tour Ford's Theater before it closed at 5 p.m. Just over four miles separate the two sites.

Seated in the back seat of my parents' car, I turned the map upside down to look in the same direction we were headed from the monastery and guided him. We arrived in enough time to visit both Ford's Theater and the house where President Lincoln died.

~~~~~

Fast forward nearly three decades when I was heading to the Greater Pittsburgh International Airport to join Duquesne University classmates on a 5:45 p.m. flight to London, where we would start a 10-day tour of England, Scotland and Wales.

This was before 9/11, so airport security wasn't nearly as intensive as it is today. Still, even though it was Sunday (so less traffic around Pittsburgh), I left my house before 1 p.m. for what should have been less than a two-and-a-half-hour trip. The Fort Pitt Bridge was under construction, so I wanted to allow myself enough time.

The drive went smoothly until soon after I exited the Squirrel Hill Tunnel to find a traffic bottleneck on the Parkway East (weekday commuters are used to a bottleneck well before the Squirrel Hill Tunnel). The longer we inched along, the more nervous I became about missing my flight and my first extended vacation in eight years.

I was in the left lane, and on a whim decided to take the next left exit to downtown Pittsburgh in hopes I would find a quicker way onto the Fort Pitt Bridge.

And so I did; however, I could not merge into the lanes for the Fort Pitt Tunnel toward the airport, and had to exit toward Route 51. I meandered a bit, trying to follow my nose, when I saw a way to return to the highway past the tunnel.

I arrived at the airport at 4 p.m. I parked in the long-term lot and rushed to catch a tram to the terminal. I met a couple from Greensburg, about an hour east of Pittsburgh, who were scheduled on a 4:45 p.m. flight to Mexico. Like me, they had been concerned about construction on the Fort Pitt Bridge, but a friend who was a state trooper told them not to worry on a Sunday.

I hope they made their flight. I made mine, but not before seeing a sigh of relief from one of my professors, who was leading the tour with his wife, son and daughter-in-law.

I later learned that I was lucky to have avoided the Fort Pitt Tunnel. Another student, who has asthma, was stuck in the tunnel for a couple hours.

But, like Blanche DuBois in **A Streetcar Named Desire,** at times I've had no choice than to depend upon the kindness of strangers to help me get from Point A to Point B.

For example, during a 1988 tour around France when we had a rest stop, I think, in Toulouse. I became hopelessly disoriented. A kind *vieille femme* ("old woman" sounds so much better in French…

but then, doesn't everything?) understood my rudimentary French and frantic pointing at a map to take me by the hand and point me in the correct direction of our tour bus.

~~~~~

On a somewhat related note, I also advise readers not to talk in public with imaginary friends – even when you're a kid.

Probably because I was an only child, I made up an imaginary friend before I went to kindergarten. I named him "Popeye," even though I hated spinach at the time. (Even today, I eat spinach only when it's raw in a salad or combined with other ingredients in a quiche or casserole.)

Of course, Popeye went along when I accompanied my parents when they went house hunting. When I turned and said to thin air, "What do you think, Popeye?", well, it was time for mom to take me aside and gently suggest, "Marianne, maybe next time when we go out, we should leave Popeye at home."

Poor little guy didn't get to go anywhere.

Don't touch that

When I was a kid and went shopping with mom or we visited family and friends, I knew better to touch anything, especially anything fragile. You break it, you bought it (or replaced it). Wise guidance, since I'm a klutz, and I didn't get a large allowance.

When I was a kid, about the only toilet mom let me sit on was my very own potty chair.

At the top of mom's "no touching" list are public toilets. If nature called when we were out in public, mom taught me to lay folded-over strips of toilet paper over the toilet seat and straddle over the toilet for "Number One" and to be sure I sat on the toilet paper, leaning forward so as to not touch the toilet, if I had to do "Number Two."

Being a klutz, I usually knocked one or both strips of toilet paper into the toilet bowl, then had to start all over again – or risk picking up germs, cooties, and who knows what else.

If mom had seen some of the bathrooms and toilets I had no option but to use during my travels outside the United States, well, she would have added that worry to her fear of bedbugs and that my plane would crash in the ocean, my body never to be seen again.

    Women have outnumbered men on any tour I've taken. Tour coordinators usually asked us to avoid using the bathroom on the bus unless it was an emergency, in order to limit odors and clean up required each evening. Women generally take longer than men in the bathroom, so, after the last man in our group departed the men's room at a rest stop, a woman would station herself outside the men's room so that the rest of us could relieve ourselves.

    The public bathrooms, fittingly also known as "pissoirs," smelled awful and had paper and water on the floor. Maybe it was water. They were worse than any porta john I've ever used. Whenever possible, I "held it" until I could use the bathroom at the next site we were scheduled to tour.

    On one tour, during a lunch stop in a small British town, I couldn't wait. I found the public toilet, which consisted of a series of holes in the ground. No seat. No flush control. No toilet paper. No privacy. (NOTE TO FUTURE TRAVELERS: ALWAYS, BUT ALWAYS, CARRY TISSUES ON YOU.)

    This happened six years before our parish organized on a trip to Croatia and Slovenia, ancestral homeland of the founders of our church. Our trip was wonderful, including tours of Dubrovnik, Opatija, Split, Trogir, Zadar and Zagreb in Croatia, and Bled, Ljubljana and Postojna in Slovenia.

    One afternoon, we hiked and boated in the Plitvice Lakes National Park, which is a UNESCO-protected site. The Park's turquoise lakes and numerous waterfalls provide a postcard-worthy scene at every turn. I wish I had worn a pedometer, because we walked for at least three hours, resulting in the best sleep I've ever experienced away from home. It was late September, so as the temperature dropped, most of us needed a comfort stop (remember, we saw and heard a lot of waterfalls). As other female travelers and I entered the rest facility, I wasn't surprised at what we found out in the middle of nature. Yep, a row of holes in the ground.

Well, you'd think the rest of the women had seen the Pope. Or a movie star. Anyone famous. They whipped out their cameras and took photos – fortunately, before any of us dropped their drawers.

I saved my film for the lakes and waterfalls.

~~~~~

Another touching no-no was popping my pimples. I've experienced acne outbreaks for more than four decades, less frequently as an adult, but acne just the same. Unfortunately, I often ignore mom's advice and squeeze away. Usually not a good decision.

In my sixth decade, I've realized I have a love/hate relationship with my oily-combination skin inherited from dad's side of the family. The same complexion type that causes acne outbreaks also helps to reduce wrinkles.

Mom's side of the family possessed great complexion genes. My mom is usually believed to be a decade younger than she is. My Uncle Joe Lugar perhaps had the best skin – he looked at least 20 years younger than his 91 years when he died.

Don't talk money, family business, politics or religion with people you don't know well (and mind your own business)

When I was a kid, you just didn't talk about these things, especially if you had no idea what you were talking about.

From 1959 to 1975, WTAE-TV, Pittsburgh, aired a children's television show called **Adventure Time**. Paul Shannon was the host, assisted by guitarist Joe Negri and puppeteer Jim Martin, who later worked on **Sesame Street**. The show featured cartoons and old Three Stooges short films (Wikipedia).

At some point when I watched the show, Paul Shannon was off for an extended period of time. Nick Perry, who later hosted the televised drawings of the Pennsylvania Lottery – and was imprisoned for masterminding the Triple Six Fix plot to rig The Daily Number drawing – served as temporary host.

One evening my parents wondered if Shannon was on vacation, or sick. Repeating a word I had heard, but didn't understand other than it referred to some illness, I replied, "Maybe he has cancer."

You'd think I had said, "There is no God."

My parents shushed me and told me never to say such a bad thing, not to talk like that about something I knew nothing about, not to spread unfounded rumors.

How I wish that rule pertained to social media today. Our country and world would be a much more civil and polite place.

On a sad note, Paul Shannon did pass away from brain cancer in 1990 while living in retirement in Florida **(Pittsburgh Post-Gazette,** July 26, 1990).

~~~~~

When we visited with family and friends, my parents reminded me not to discuss our personal business – and also to mind my own business. That meant not asking prying questions, and not snooping around others' homes on my own.

Mind you, visitors to our house didn't always share my parents' views on personal space and boundaries.

My lifelong aversion to "dropping in" on people without warning dates back to my childhood. It just wasn't polite. You call first and schedule a visit.

And during visits to other homes, no snooping around in rooms unless the host is conducting a tour. If I had to use the bathroom, I asked where it was located, then fitted myself with imaginary blinders so I wouldn't look in other rooms I passed on my way to and from the bathroom.

~~~~~

During my tenure as a communications manager, aka spokesperson, for the American Red Cross, I did not discuss politics publicly. I did not make political comments on Facebook from the time I joined the social network in 2009 until after I retired from the Red Cross in early 2015. I've never displayed a candidate's "stick in the ground" sign in my yard, nor have I displayed any political signage, such as bumper stickers or campaign pins.

I acted in this manner partly because of how I was raised and because the Red Cross is a neutral organization. I was concerned that even though I had individual rights to take a political stand "on my own time," since the public saw me as the official Red Cross representative, some might confuse my views with that of the organization.

I'm not saying I never discussed politics at work. I did so rarely – but in private, behind closed doors, usually with like-minded individuals. Even today, I comment less on political policy on Facebook than I do on behaviors and social justice issues (as in those related to Christ's teachings, including The Golden Rule and the Beatitudes). And I avoid such comments on Twitter, which I've used primarily for my freelance work.

I scratch my head at social media contacts who combine their sales business and politics in the same social media feed.

Even though in my semi-retirement role as a freelance correspondent I mainly write features and columns, I will not display political signage at my home, on my car, or on my person.

I remember an assignment when I conducted an interview in the subject's home. As we were nearing the end of the interview, out of the blue the subject asked me what I thought of a newly-elected official. Since I was raised not to lie, I've never been able to keep a poker face, so I'm sure my shock (and maybe even displeasure at the official) showed. I demurred, saying something like, "I don't discuss politics or my views in my job." I was mortified.

~~~~~

I was raised to believe actions speak louder than words. Especially when it comes to matters of faith, I try to adhere to the quote popularly attributed to Saint Francis of Assisi: "Preach the Gospel at all times and if necessary, use words."

So, you won't find me proselytizing on street corners or going door-to-door selling my religion. Instead I try to live my faith in how I treat others and support community needs through charitable giving and service, using "The Golden Rule" and "The Beatitudes" as my moral compasses.

Several years ago, when I worked in downtown Johnstown, members of a fundamentalist denomination often proselytized on a corner of Central Park. I usually avoided them, but during one lunch break my mind must have been miles away because I found myself walking toward an adult man and youth shouting on the corner.

I figured they'd scream just the same if I turned around and walked in the opposite direction, so I continued on and tried to mind my own business.

The pair yelled, telling me I had to repent, then asked which religion I followed. I answered, "I'm a Roman Catholic."

That set them both off, and the preteen was worse than the adult in insulting my faith and its practitioners. They told me I was destined for Hell.

I replied that my God, my Christ, is about LOVE, not hate and punishment. They kept yelling, and I repeated myself, and went on my way, not looking back.

~~~~~

Last, but not least, don't expect any "kiss and tell" narratives about my romantic life in this book. Such content falls under the category of family business, and that remains private.

Don't say "never" or "always"

Why? "Never" and "Always" are too long of a time period, at least when you're talking about the future. Looking back at the past, "always" and "never" are certainly acceptable, if true.

The focus of my mother's precautionary tale for this one? Debbie Reynolds.

Mom and I share a fondness for old movies, particularly those from Hollywood's Golden Age of the 1930s through 1950s. Over the years, she's often reminded me of what she recalls Reynolds having said after she married Eddie Fisher in 1955: "We'll always be together."

Four years later, Reynolds and Fisher had divorced in the wake of Fisher's relationship with Elizabeth Taylor following the death of her third husband, Mike Todd, who had been a good friend of Fisher.

Some "always" and "never" statements are just plain wrong. No matter what Forrest Gump says ("Mama always said that life was like a box of chocolates… you never know what you're going to get").

Having eaten a couple hundred pounds of chocolate over the years, I know that my favorite chocolate shop swirls a "B" atop butter creams, an "S" atop strawberry creams, an "R" atop raspberry creams, and an "M" atop maple nut creams (ugh). Wet coconut candies come in red paper cups. Peanut butter candies have a long narrow swirl and come in brown paper cups.

Still, I'm all for keeping a few famous "always" lines.

"We'll always have Paris" stated by Rick to Ilsa in **Casablanca.**

"Always" by Irving Berlin.

"I will always love you" as sung by Whitney Houston.

If your friends jumped in the lake, would you?

Being an introvert, I usually didn't hang out with a group. I had friends, but few that I would consider "bosom buddies."

Maybe that's why I tended not to follow the crowd. I may have come of age in the 1970s, but I've never smoked. I've never done drugs. I didn't party. Even now, I seldom drink alcohol. Yeah, I'm pretty boring.

One of my close friends started to smoke to impress a boy who smoked. I thought that was a silly thing to do, to risk one's health in that way.

I followed the example of my parents, who didn't smoke or do drugs, and drank alcohol only occasionally.

When it comes to clothes, I've seldom followed fads, instead favoring fashion classics – with a few exceptions.

For example, platform shoes. My goodness, those were uncomfortable. I remember wearing a pair when I worked in the advertising department of our local newspaper during the summer. One day when I returned some proofs to the composing department, I slid and fell out of my shoes and onto my posterior – all while wearing a dress.

High heels and pointed toe shoes – uncomfortable AND difficult to walk on, even without ever wearing spiked heels. Over time, even two-inch heels were too high. Now I seldom wear heels higher than an inch.

Fish net stockings. They didn't keep you warm, and made you look like a walk-on in a high school production of **Caberet,** the model for the infamous leg lamp in **A Christmas Story,** or, worse yet, employed in the world's oldest profession.

Jackets with wide lapels. I learned too late that they made me look even bustier. Plus, the extra-large lapels usually wrinkled in the closet.

Wearing sneakers with office garb on errands and between home and work? Now that's a fad worth keeping.

Don't suck your thumb

Like many kids, I sucked my thumb. But I wonder how many kids sucked their thumb past their fourth birthday?

My parents thought it was cute that I sucked my thumb when I was an infant. With each passing year, mom tried to get me to stop.

Caught in the act of sucking my thumb.

If she heard me while she was in another part of the apartment, she told me to stop. She started telling me that I was going to ruin my teeth. Didn't matter.

After my third birthday, mom took more aggressive action. She put hot sauce on my thumb. Teary-eyed and crying, I kept right on sucking. After about two weeks, mom gave up, although she still worried that I would continue to suck my thumb in kindergarten and into adulthood.

What has lasted into adulthood is my tolerance for hot, spicy food – Cajun, Mexican, Chinese (Szechuan style) and Indian. I've seldom met a spicy food I haven't tried – and usually enjoyed.

Months before my fourth birthday, we moved from the

apartment my parents had rented since their marriage to a duplex. Six months later, we moved to the home where mom still lives.

Looking back on our time living in the duplex, mom recalls how unhappy I seemed living somewhere new. I settled in more easily in a home of our own. Not long after we moved in, mom told my dad that she hadn't seen or heard me sucking my thumb for a couple of weeks.

Lucky for me, I had stopped cold turkey a few months starting kindergarten.

Don't wish your life away

When I was a kid, I would sometimes wish I was older. For example, "I wish I were 16 so I could drive" or "I wish it was Christmas."

Or, once I started to travel, "I wish it was (insert date) and I would be on my way."

Mom would respond, "Don't wish your life away."

I dreaded turning 30. I wasn't married, had no children, unlike most of my classmates.

Hitting 40 wasn't so bad. If I hadn't pretty much accepted the fact that I wouldn't have kids, my having a severe case of endometriosis, requiring a hysterectomy, then being diagnosed with Stage I Ovarian Cancer dramatically slammed the door on any remaining hopes of having offspring.

Having survived cancer changed my perspective on a lot of things, including my life priorities. Instead of dwelling on what I didn't have, I've consciously tried to focus on what I do have – the many blessings in my life.

But you could still catch me looking ahead to the future, to some degree.

After I turned 50, my birthday mantra became, "Another year closer to retirement."

Since I retired from my full-time job, it's now, "Another year closer to Social Security."

Don't get a fat Christmas tree - but do use white lights

According to my mom, I've loved Christmas ever since I was a kid. One of her favorite photos of me was taken one Christmas morning after I had raced to our tree and kissed the glittery snow blanket roll that mom had laid underneath the tree.

Having grown up during the Great Depression, my mom always wanted a better life for me. When it came to Christmas, that included having my picture taken with Santa Claus every year from when I was 1 through age 6 – before every Christmas when I believed in Santa Claus.

I was a smiling, happy toddler for my first photo with Santa. The following year? I was in my terrible twos. I cried and cried and cried. Mom was so embarrassed. Santa's helpers assured her not to worry, that I would grow out of it the following year. And so I did.

For varied reasons, Christmas wasn't always a happy time. But even during those sad holiday seasons, I wanted to help put up the Christmas tree, bake cookies and wrap gifts.

And I always wanted a real Christmas tree. My parents bought an artificial tree after mom went back to work full-time. I hated it. After a while, when too many old-fashioned sharp bristle "needles" started falling out, we went back to a real tree.

~~~~~

When I bought a real tree for my first Christmas my first home, I bought a fat tree. The tree was so fat, it took up about one-eighth of my living room. I continued to buy fat trees just about every year in that house.

Because of the size of the trees I bought, they had to be placed in a corner. You couldn't walk around them in any room in my first house. My parents usually helped me stand the tree. Dad and I would carry the tree in from my garage, then he would try to hold it steady in the tree stand as mom watched to make sure it stayed straight while I tightened the screws into the tree.

One year, the evening after we placed the tree in its corner of the living room, I was writing out Christmas cards in the dining room when I heard a rustling sound, then WHOOSH… CRASH…TINKLE.

I rushed to the living room to see that my beautifully decorated Christmas tree HAD FALLEN OVER!

I started bawling. I couldn't lift the tree back myself, so I called my parents and through hysterical sobs told them what happened. They came to my house, and mom told me to pick up the ornaments I could before my dad and I stood the tree again. We placed more magazines under the stand to help keep the tree standing straight and tall.

Surprisingly, no ornaments had been lost. The couple resin ornaments that had broken could be glued back together. Amazingly, the few blown glass ornaments I had – including one from my godmother, my Aunt Donna (and mom's baby sister) – were intact. It appeared they were protected among the soft branches inside which they had been placed. As for the rest, perhaps the living room carpeting helped break the fall.

During the 16 holiday seasons I lived at my first home, my big, fat Christmas tree fell over two more times, different years. We figured all the ornaments placed on three sides of the trees made the tree unbalanced and top-heavy.

After the third time, we wised up and dad installed a large hook in the corner; after we stood the tree, we would wrap rope around its trunk, about halfway up the tree, then wrap the rope around the hook and tie it tight. The hook indeed put an end to my tipsy trees, but it probably caused a few raised eyebrows when I sold my first house. After Christmas, the tree came down, but the hook stayed.

My current house has two small open staircases, five steps from the family room to dining room, and four steps from the living room to the main bathroom, guest bedroom and office.

By this time, I had accumulated enough penguin ornaments to decorate a second tree (I started collecting penguin figurines, ornaments, etc., in the late 1980s). My first Christmas in my new home, I managed to find a narrow real tree to place next to the family room staircase, which is located about six feet from the door to the garage and four feet from a large recliner chair I inherited from my Uncle Fred, who had been widowed after my Aunt Donna's death.

The following year, I broke down and bought a nice artificial tree for the family room. But I still had to put a real tree next to the staircase in my living room. After we placed the real tree, I would wrap a rope around the trunk, then around the top of the railing.

Imagine my disbelief when one year while I had a few coworkers over for dinner, the tree in the living room fell over. Water was flowing over my nice hardwood floors. A few ornaments, including my glass ***It's a Wonderful Life*** ornament, had broken on my non-carpeted floors.

I figured out that I had placed the rope too low. In subsequent years, I wrapped TWO ropes around the tree, one about a third the way up the trunk and the other about two-thirds up the trunk.

And yes, my friends helped me clean up the mess.

~~~~~

One of my and my mom's longest-running disagreements centers on white lights vs. colored lights. She much prefers white lights, while I like colored lights.

Before we purchased our first artificial tree, we decorated our real trees with strands of old-fashioned light bulbs. For several years, mom used a white/red/gold color scheme on our artificial tree: white lights, red satin balls and gold tinsel (BORING if you ask me).

I took the old Shiny Brite ornaments to use on the four-foot artificial tree I put up in my bedroom. I also got custody of the Christmas village houses my parents used to put under the tree.

By the time we went back to putting up a real tree, the red satin balls had frayed, and the gold tinsel was less tinny. We used an assortment of ornaments, but the white lights remained.

Acquiescing to my age, I recently purchased a high-quality 7.5-foot artificial tree for the living room – on sale at a 60 percent discount. The tree comes with nine light settings: steady warm white, steady multicolor, fading warm white, fading multicolor, flashing warm white, flashing multicolor, slowly flashing warm white to multicolor, quickly flashing warm white to multicolor – and warm white fading to multicolor.

A Christmas tree lights compromise for mom and me!

Even though my mom (and dad) hadn't put up a Christmas tree for years, she helps me with my tree every year. She unpackages ornaments for me to hang on my two trees, then packages them back up (more neatly than I would, I must add). It's one of our most-cherished traditions.

Please Do...

Pick up after yourself and put things back where you found them

If I recall correctly, my earliest lesson on this subject occurred when I was in middle school. My parents were at work, and I decided to bake a cake all by myself for the first time. It must have slipped my mind that we didn't have a maid, because I left the ingredients and dirty bowls, pans and utensils on the kitchen counter and table.

My parents loved the cake, but hated the mess. Mom told me that I could bake or cook whatever I wanted, but I had to clean up after myself and put supplies back where I found them.

Coming from a family of eight, mom had plenty of chores to do when she was growing up. She always wanted better for me, so I wasn't expected to help her keep house, except for setting the table and washing dishes. She washed my clothes and did my ironing while I lived with my parents, and even did most of my spring housecleaning for several years after she retired from the sewing factory.

However, I was expected to keep my bedroom in order: make the bed, hang up my clothes, keep my drawers neat, polish my shoes, etc.

When I was a teenager, I began helping mom with spring housecleaning during my summer vacation. I polished furniture and washed walls and the fancy dishes and glasses in the china closet. I was also expected to wash my car and keep it clean.

We often joked that our floor was so clean that you could eat off it.

After I bought my first house, she was concerned that I would struggle in maintaining the house. But I had observed well and had a good teacher.

I do a pretty good job keeping my house tidy, even following mom's spring housecleaning tradition. I even iron my window sheers.

Then we have the family room and basement. Let's say the family room looks "lived in." As for the basement, well, no one except me goes there.

In fairness, as my mom has been slowed down by pain in her back, neck and knees, she's told me she wished she hadn't spent so much time cleaning her house. A neat house, yes. A spotless house, no.

~~~~~

I can't watch **Snow White and the Seven Dwarfs** or **The Wizard of Oz** without remembering the snarky comments my mom has made during both films ever since I was a kid.

Birds and critters helping Snow White clean up after the dwarfs? Yeah, right! More like making more dirt, leaving droppings and poop all over the place.

Winged monkeys? Just imagine all the poop they drop everywhere.

When we watch Macy's Thanksgiving Day Parade and Tournament of Roses Parade, mom has always paid more attention to the people cleaning up after than the equestrian units than the beautiful floats and talented marching bands.

~~~~~

The one person who could get away with not putting things back where she found them – even messing up mom's orderly linen drawers – was my cousin Suzie. Each time she and my Aunt Donna and Uncle Fred dined with us, Suzie would invariably

My Cousin Suzie holds my dog, Mitzi, as we take a break during a game of Twister.

unfold and mix up my mom's neatly folded dish towels when we started washing dishes. It was a running joke between my mom and my cousin, and made mom laugh every time.

You get what you pay for…and take care of your investment

Long before my mom was engaged to my dad, the husband of a friend of hers sold her a set of Magnalite cast aluminum pots and pans.

Over the course of six decades, she and my dad replaced their roof twice, furnace twice, hot water tank three times, and major appliances at least two times.

Her set of Magnalite pots and pans remain in great shape.

Long before I bought my first house, mom started my porcelain nativity set (new pieces every year from Avon) and my set of Magnalite pots and pans. My cookware includes an 11.5-inch high wall frying pan, an 8-quart roaster, 7.5-quart and 6-quart Dutch ovens, 4-quart and 3-quart pots, and two 1.5 quart saucepans – almost all with their own lids.

The current purchase price of my Magnalite cookware? Based on pricing on Amazon for Magnalite's current line, I'd estimate well over $600.

Until I retired from my full-time job in January of 2015, I'm certain I used the nativity set more often than most of my Magnalite cookware. I used the saucepan the most, to melt butter to make pizzelles before having instructions how to soften and melt butter using my microwave oven.

But as I started doing most of the cooking for mom and me, I was sure glad I had such high-quality, sturdy cookware.

Two years into my semi-retirement, I asked mom if she would give me the Magnalite pot she used to cook potatoes before mashing. This pot is wider and shorter than my other pots. Although there's no volume marked on the bottom, I'd say it's about 2.5 quarts, which is ideal when I need a pot slightly larger than a sauce pan.

~~~~~

After my Grandma Lugar died, I asked for three items from her house: a pair of grape-shaped plaster sconces and two cookie sheets (also known as jelly roll pans) she used to bake her famous apple strudel.

The sconces were a kitschy reminder of Grandma's colorful room décor.

The cookie sheets, manufactured by Nash Metalware, are thicker and heavier than any other cookie sheet I've seen. Since grandma's death in 1991, I've baked more than 500 dozen of cookies using these pans – and they're still going strong. The sides and bottoms of the pans have burned-in stains from strudel ingredients. I haven't tried to scour them. The stains stay to remind me of Grandma Lugar.

~~~~~

When I worked full-time in an office, Pendleton was one of my favorite clothing brands. I bought a dozen or more Pendleton skirts and nearly two dozen jackets. I particularly liked the plaid '49er jackets, based one of the company's designs from 1949.

I bought my first 49er jacket in 2001, and I'm still wearing it. The wool fabric hasn't pilled or shown any evidence of wear.

I've had the same experience with jewelry. Instead of buying several gold-plated pieces that tarnish over time, I'd rather buy one piece of 14k gold or other quality pieces.

Perhaps pantyhose is an exception to mom's saying. Whether you buy stockings for $1 or $6 a pair, they will snag and run eventually. I've often said that scientists have concocted a formula for nylons that won't run and automobiles that won't rust, but our government, realizing the negative impact such formulas would have on our economy, has locked them up in the same storage facility as the Ark of the Covenant.

Just my theory, mind you.

~~~~~

It seems that I go through umbrellas like some people go through chewing gum. I try to carefully close and secure them, but it doesn't take long for the ribs to bend and loosen.

I've lost more than my fair share of umbrellas. The most memorable incident occurred during my junior year of college. I had an umbrella that I had carried across Europe for two weeks.

One rainy day, when I arrived at the classroom, I saw that class was still in session. I sat on the bench outside the door and placed the umbrella on the bench. When class ended, I rose and walked in the classroom, but left the umbrella behind. I realized it as soon as I got to my desk, but when I returned to the bench, I saw that someone had already taken it.

Chocolate makes your face break out

I inherited my sweet tooth from my dad. When it comes to the Aztecs' "food of the gods," I've seldom met a chocolate I haven't tried – or enjoyed.

Diabetes runs in my mom's family. Although the "sweets" gene seems to be recessive in my mom, my Grandpa Lugar enjoyed his sweets, particularly ice cream. Both Grandma and Grandpa Lugar took medications to control their diabetes. So far, my mom hasn't been diagnosed, but she watches her diet just the same.

When I was a teen, she was concerned about chocolate making my face break out. I may be nearing the end of my sixth decade, but at times my face seems lost back in my teens (although I seem to have a greater reaction to potato chips and other fatty foods).

Reminding me of my Lugar genes, now mom is more concerned about my being diagnosed with diabetes in the future, despite my glucose level remaining in normal levels.

As previously mentioned, I rarely drink alcohol. I've never smoked or taken recreational drugs. So let me eat chocolate.

Get plenty of rest
Mom did definitely inherit the Lugar "nod off" gene.

She and I have two movie-watching traditions. Each D-Day Anniversary, we watch **The Longest Day**. Then on Independence Day, we watch **1776**.

At least half the time when I look over at mom during the movies, she's nodded off. She inevitably must watch new episodes of her favorite television shows a couple of times to view the episode in its entirety.

Since my dad was known to fall asleep while reading the newspaper, it would seem I may have a double dose of the "nap" gene. I typically don't feel drowsy while reading the newspaper or watching television or a movie. Instead, I usually nod off while I'm saying my morning prayers – and after enjoying a carbs-loaded meal. Working crossword puzzles and reading a book when I go to bed also usually make me drowsy.

But give me a couple more decades and I'll probably fall asleep in front of the television.

With your naturally curly hair, you should wear your hair short

Look at my currently thick head of hair, and you'd never think that I hardly had any hair when I was born. My dad's older sister, Connie, gave birth to my Cousin Ray the day after mom had me. In the photo, she's holding Ray on the left while my mom holds me. If not for my wearing a dress, many might assume that my mom was holding a boy and my Aunt Connie, a girl.

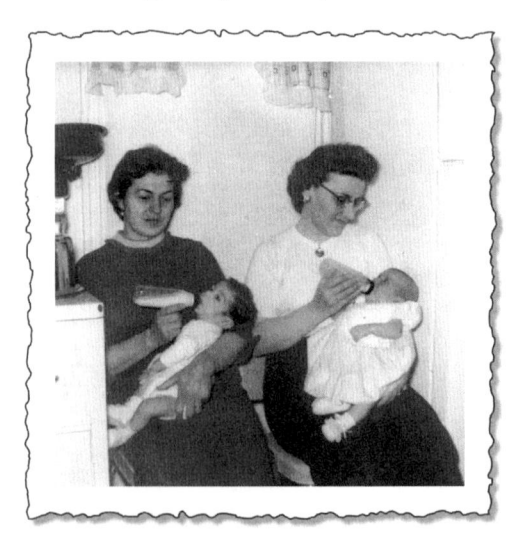

At left, Aunt Connie holds my Cousin Ray while mom holds me.

Although he was only 50 percent Italian, my dad had the dark, curly hair associated with Italians. (Ironically, Grandpa Spampinato's sister married a *paisan* with fair coloring; they had six children – three with dark coloring, three with fair coloring.)

My mom had straight hair, so, like many of her generation, went to the beauty salon a couple times a year to have her hair styled in a permanent wave.

My hair really started coming in after my first birthday. As was the fashion for my generation who came of age in the 1960s and 1970s, I wanted to wear my naturally wavy hair long, below my shoulders, frizzes and all.

I wore my hair long and stringy for my eighth-grade class photo...

I was tired of mom saying, "If I had your hair, I would have it cut in a short style to show off those curls. All you're doing with that long hair is stretching out the curl."

In my official high school and college portraits, my curly hair touches my shoulders. During my senior year of high school, I wore a shag cut. Around this time, the Dorothy Hamill cut became the rage, so some of my classmates started wearing shorter hair. I soon joined them, most likely because it took a lot less time to get ready in the morning.

From left to right in this holiday photo when I was in my 20s: Grandma Lugar, mom and dad, with me in front. Mom gave Grandma Lugar perms and had her hair permed; dad had naturally curly hair. My shorter haircut shows off my natural wavy hair.

~~~~~

I was still in high school when I found my first gray hair. I was shocked, but my parents weren't surprised. Their hair was gradually turning gray as they aged. However, my dad's brother Joe turned nearly all gray in his 20s.

I consoled myself that having gray hair was better than going bald, as my mom's brother Joe did in his 30s.

When my gray hair became too noticeable, I started using temporary hair color that lasted for a week. It became my Sunday morning ritual, much to my mom's chagrin. Even temporary hair color may stain towels so much that the dark spots may never come out. On her request, I used the same stained towels over and over again.

Around the time I bought my first house, I switched to a hair salon closer to what would become my new neighborhood. I started having my hair dyed at the salon whenever I went for a haircut. A few years too late for mom's towels.

~~~~~

After I was diagnosed with cancer in 2001, I underwent six chemotherapy treatments. I was told my hair would start falling out about two weeks after my initial treatment. Friends who underwent the same chemotherapy regimen told me the same thing.

As my doctor's staff recommended, I was fitted for two wigs before my first treatment, but wasn't convinced I would need them. I thought about using a head covering instead of a wig, but was concerned that when I did television interviews, viewers would pay more attention to my appearance than what I was saying.

A hundred similar predictions couldn't prepare me for what

happened when I washed my hair two weeks (to the day) after starting chemotherapy. My body told me it was going to happen – my scalp had been tender for a couple days – but my mind wasn't convinced until I saw a pile of my hair in the sink.

Ted, my supervisor at the time, phoned me once a week following my surgery and recovery. He had the dumb luck to call me the day my hair started falling out.

"Sob…Hi, Ted…sob..sob…sniff…thanks for calling…sob…sniff…"

Over the years, I've often said that Ted deserved sainthood, if only for putting up with me and keeping his composure the day I started losing my hair.

Others who underwent the same chemotherapy regimen will likely tell you that their hair started growing in before the end of their treatments. Just a stubble, but the hair was coming in. But then their eyebrows and eyelashes started falling out.

Five months after my hair fell out, the borough where my parents lived was having a family portrait fundraiser. A family posed for group and individual photos, then the borough shared in the proceeds from orders of portrait packets.

In my photo for the photo package fundraiser conducted by the borough where my parents lived, I was still wearing a wig and had no eyebrows or eyelashes.

I had neither eyebrows nor eyelashes. I drew in eyebrows, but despite having purchased false eyelashes, never attempted to put them on.

Mom was curious how gray my hair was – at this point I probably had dyed it for two decades – and asked me to hold off having it dyed until she could look at my head of newly grown hair.

I replied that it wasn't going to grow two inches overnight. Besides, my hair stylist wanted my hair to become stronger before dying it. When my parents looked at the stubby hair on my head, they saw it was about half white and half dark brown.

My hair was strong enough to be dyed by late spring the following year.

My hair started falling out around Father's Day in 2001. It was fully grown in, kinky as a lamb's, for Mother's Day in 2002.

Wear clean underwear – you never know when you'll be in an accident

If I recall correctly, I've been in five automobile accidents, of which I was fully at fault for only two, although all of the accidents required car repair. I've been driving for more than 40 years, so having been at fault for one accident every 20 years is pretty good.

Plus, there was one fake accident. When I was a senior in high school, our school was invited to participate in a disaster drill. I played a student injured when her school bus was in an accident.

We made the local newspaper. My cameo appearance in the coverage? This paragraph, midway in the article: "Another girl, in the heat and confusion of the bus interior, fainted and was revived with smelling salts."

Fortunately, none of these incidents resulted in anyone but me seeing that I was wearing clean underwear. Likewise, I was lucky to never have an "accident" when I was in an accident.

Oh, there was the time when I was in kindergarten that I pooped my pants and I had to walk home wearing no underwear for six blocks. I thought I had a little flatulence. Wrong.

Girls usually wore dresses to school back then, so if I had seen **The Seven Year Itch** at such a tender age, I would have felt like Marilyn Monroe straddling the subway grate.

~~~~~

Most of my automobile accidents were memorable for other reasons.

I attribute the first accident, which happened more than three decades ago, to being absent-minded. I had taken my Grandma Lugar grocery shopping and apparently didn't close the rear hatch of my car properly. I thought it seemed unusually breezy in my two-door Plymouth Horizon, but didn't pull over to check it out.

Then I started to back my car into my parents' garage. CRUNCH!

My second accident wasn't that unusual. Another car and I backed out of our parking spaces at a local shopping center at the same time, but couldn't see each other in our vehicle's blind spot. CRASH. Our rear bumpers collided, but fortunately, we weren't going fast, so relatively little damage. After this accident, I avoided that narrow throughway – and started backing into parking spaces more often.

The third accident happened in 2006 and involved my 2002 Dodge Stratus. I had taken my car to the local dealership for annual inspection on a day off, then was driven home, where I worked on my income taxes.

Working on my taxes apparently made my head go numb because I left my checkbook and driver's license at home on the dining room table when I was given a ride to pick up my car.

I was driving home on a moderately busy street to pick up those items then return to the dealership when I had to stop behind a car that was stopped behind another car waiting to turn left.

As we waited (the front car passed up several opportunities to turn), I looked in my rear-view mirror and saw another car rapidly approaching. I didn't think it would be able to stop in time. Just after the lead car finally turned left and the car in front of me drove on, my car was rear-ended.

No witnesses. Even worse, I didn't have a current driver's license on me, although I still carried my previous license in my wallet.

I yelled at the other driver, "How could you not see my car?

We'd been stopped for a while. I know my brake lights work, because my car just passed inspection!"

"I had something in my eye and couldn't see," the other driver replied.

A police officer came, took our statements, and even though the other driver was at fault, I thought I would also be in trouble for not having my current license on me. However, the officer confirmed my current license status and let it go after hearing my explanation.

In taking responsibility for the accident, the other driver also told the officer more than she had told me. "She said she was smoking a cigarette and an ash got in her eye," the officer told me.

Fortunately, the damage didn't prevent me from driving the car until it could be repaired.

Same for my fourth accident.

I had my 2011 Subaru Legacy sedan for about four months when I was taking my parents to a basket party fundraiser at a church hall about 15 miles away.

I was driving on a two-lane road when I saw what I thought was a crazed dog running wildly down a hill and onto the road, heading in my car's general direction. I started to slow down, considered driving to the side of the road, but thought better of it considering the animal's unpredictable movements.

I saw in my rear-view mirror that the car behind me saw what was happening, and also slowed down. Both of our cars came to a nearly complete stop.

The animal, which on closer examination was the mangiest, ugliest dog that I have ever seen, hit my left front headlight area.

When I've shared this experience with my friends, many asked at this point of the story, "What happened to the animal?!?!"

"IT BOUNCED OFF MY CAR AND RAN BACK UP THE

HILL WHERE IT CAME FROM!" I replied, "AND CAUSED $500 IN DAMAGES TO MY FOG LIGHT ASSEMBLY!"

Other friends have suggested that it was a coyote, not a dog, that hit my car.

BEEP BEEP!! I'm not with the Acme car dealership. And my car in no way resembles a road runner.

In my travels on behalf of the American Red Cross, I've driven home from Philadelphia in a rain storm that transitioned to snow in the higher elevation of central Pennsylvania (and fortunately found myself behind a PennDOT truck from the time it entered the turnpike at the Blue Mountain Tunnel until it exited the turnpike 30 miles later at the Tuscarora Tunnel). I've driven home from Harrisburg in a sleet storm. Yet I never had an accident in wet or dry road conditions.

One Sunday in late January of 2014, I had picked up my parents to take them to church, out for Sunday dinner, then home. My dad hadn't driven in about four years because of some medications and having been diagnosed with mild Parkinson's disease. Mom has never driven in wintry weather.

A wet snow was falling, but it wasn't snowing heavily.

Mom reminded me to call them when I returned home to let them know that I had safety completed my four-mile trip home.

As I neared my home, the snow picked up a bit as I ascended a hill, but the roads were slushy at worst.

And, I assured myself, I had an all-wheel drive Subaru.

About seven blocks away from my house, I slowed down to make a left turn as I continued up a slight hill.

My car, however, kept going straight, heading for the guy-wire attached to the telephone pole at the corner. I took my foot off the gas, but didn't brake, hoping the car would stop.

It did, but not before hitting the guy-wire, causing more than

$2,000 in damage to my hood, grille and front bumper. The rear right side of my car, which includes my gas tank, came to a stop about an inch away from the telephone pole.

All I can figure is that I had hit a patch of black ice. I watched for traffic and carefully backed out into the street, avoiding the telephone pole.

When I returned home, I was amazed that I was relatively calm and composed. I called my parents, and mom asked if I got home OK.

"Well, I did, I'm OK, but my car…" I replied.

Ever since, my parents stayed home when the weather was bad. The winter of 2014 was unusually bad, so I held off having the car repaired until April.

After all, if I was unlucky enough to have one winter-weather accident while driving a Subaru, I could have another one.

But at least my underwear was clean.

Wear your Sunday best

For my family, wearing your best clothes to Sunday Mass was a form of respect to our Creator. I was raised in the belief that gathering together to thank God for our blessings and pray for His comfort and strength during trials was the most important hour of each week. If you dress for success at work, dress to the nines for the theater, but are content to dress like a bum when you attend Mass, then what does that say about your life priorities?

Mom and me wearing our Easter Sunday best at Grandparents Lugars' home.

This does not mean that people should wear fancy clothing when they attend worship services. Those of means should, however, put on neat, clean and intact clothing – no holes or other indications of wear.

By the time I transferred to parochial school, where we attended Mass on holy days and Stations of the Cross during Lent, women were no longer required to wear head coverings in church. Women were also permitted to wear slacks. Girls, however, had to wear uniforms, which, back in my day, were skirts with blouses or jumpers over blouses. And yes, some nuns would make girls kneel on the floor and measure how high the hem of the uniform was above the knee and floor.

For the past several years, girls attending parochial school have been able to wear slacks. Lucky them, especially in the dead of winter.

The pastor of the church attached to the school building where I attended school from fifth through eighth grades had old-fashioned views. No matter about Vatican II; the pastor expected women to cover their heads. He refused to remove the church's communion rail or give communion to women dressed in slacks.

Many a school day when we forgot we were going to attend a church service there, girls would scrounge for head coverings – any head covering – even (slightly) used tissues.

Our special education teacher usually wore slacks, including on a day when we attended Mass. It must have been fall or winter, because she rolled up her pants, hiding them under her long coat. I wonder if the priest saw her pant legs sticking out from under her coat as she stood up and walked away from the communion rail.

~~~~~

Often, "Sunday Best" clothes require ironing. Each week when mom ironed when I was in school, she had much more ironing for my dad and me than for herself. She ironed dad's work shirts and dress shirts, plus my school blouses.

I sometimes helped with the ironing after high school, and I distinctly remember being in the middle of ironing something when I received the call from the American Red Cross to report for a physical prior to being offered a job.

At the Red Cross, I worked with several men who did their own ironing, as well as with women whose husbands did their own ironing. If I had ever married, I very well might have insisted on including "to each his or her own ironing" in our wedding vows.

Judging from this photo, it would seem I took a dislike to ironing at an early age.

I hate to iron. I rarely wear blouses, because washing a blouse is usually followed by having to iron it.

I stopped ironing my twill pants a few years ago. After I take my jeans, twill pants and chino crops out of the wash, I put them in the dryer for several minutes, then hang them up to finish drying. No shrinkage, few wrinkles.

Look in my closet and you'll find a rainbow of cotton or cotton blend turtlenecks worn in the winter and three-quarter length sleeve tops worn in the fall and early spring.

Go through my chest of drawers and you'll see a crayon box array of short-sleeved crinkle knit tops. I discovered the tops several years ago in a catalog. I love these tops. They retain their shape and remain ready to wear with or without jackets and sweaters even if you roll them up in a ball. I carefully fold them when putting them away, but if you're not into folding, you could roll them.

Roll them, fold them…as long as I don't have to iron them.

A MOM'S CLOTHING CARE TIP (provided by a mom other than mine who wishes to remain anonymous): To obscure the smell of body odor in clothing, spritz vodka on the clothing. Really.

MY MOM'S CLOTHING CARE TIP: Use lighter fluid to remove oil stains from clothing. Yes, really. Just don't wear the clothing item near open flames.

Karen, a distant cousin on my dad's side reports that milk removes ink stains (I've had success with hair spray). She also shared that gum can be removed with peanut butter or ice (to chill the gum for removal).

Tell the truth... it's easier than trying to remember a lie

Let's just say George Washington had nothing on my mom.

When my parents were first married, they rented a four-room apartment. When I was a toddler, my parents thought that we needed more space and rented a half of a duplex.

Less than six months later, my mom started hearing noises but couldn't track down the source. Then one morning she looked up at the ceiling and noticed that it was cracking – a lot. Mom talked with the landlord, who said that their son moved one of the jack posts from the basement to another rental property they owned.

"Are you crazy?!" my parents asked.

For their and my safety, they made plans to move – fast. My Grandmother Lugar said we should get our own home.

Except my parents couldn't afford the down payment, even though my dad was working two jobs at the time. Before he was hired full-time by the Postal Service, he worked days at Bethlehem Steel and evenings running collections for the Post Office.

My maternal grandparents said they would loan my parents the money. My mom agreed, on one condition – that they keep a written record of the loan and repayments.

After we settled on a house being sold by one of my dad's co-workers, my Uncle Joe drew up a paper to formalize the $1,300 loan from my grandparents to cover the down payment and closing fee.

My mom repaid my grandparents $50 each month, and each month mom dated the paper and grandmother signed to acknowledge that she had received the money.

Mom's rationale? She did not want her five siblings to think she received something that they didn't.

Each month, Grandma Lugar asked, "Could you use this money?" Especially before mom returned to work full-time, she said, "Yes, we could use it, but we would never repay the loan."

After my Grandma Lugar died in 1991 (Grandpa Lugar died in 1979), my mom showed my Uncle Joe, executor of grandma's estate, the paper indicating that the loan had been repaid in full.

With a wave of his hand, he dismissed any concerns of my mom, telling her, "If you hadn't repaid that loan, the rest of us wouldn't have heard the end of it."

~~~~~

Like my mom, my Aunt Donna (mom's youngest sister and my godmother) believed in honesty and fairness. She was intent on spending the same amount of money on gifts for my mom, dad and me. So much so that along with our gift, we'd often also receive a card, heavy from all the quarters, dimes, nickels and pennies she taped on it to make things "even Steven."

~~~~~

I've lost count of the number of times that I've been given incorrect change (usually more than I was due) and I've told the cashier about it. The cashier is always grateful, and usually surprised by my honesty.

Luke 16:10: "Whoever can be trusted with very little can also be trusted with much, and whoever is dishonest with very little will also be dishonest with much." (New International Version)

~~~~~

Several years during my tenure at the American Red Cross, I served as secretary for two community organizations, plus edited a monthly newsletter for a third organization.

These roles required me to make copies of newsletters and draft minutes, and it was more convenient to stay late and make copies at work. Every couple of months, I gave a member of our finance staff $10 to $20 to cover the cost of making copies.

The first time I handed over money to one co-worker, she was mystified and asked what it was for. I told her I wanted to cover my personal copying costs.

Stunned, she said that my "payment" was uncommon.

~~~~~

Because American Red Cross Blood Services is licensed by the U. S. Food and Drug Administration, our communications, marketing and advertising materials had to comply with federal guidelines.

For example, we could not tell a prospective blood donor that his or her donation WILL save a life. COULD save a life or MAY save a life, yes. Trauma teams may transfuse hundreds of blood products in unsuccessful efforts to save lives. Terminally ill cancer patients may receive blood products to improve their quality of life.

We could not claim to provide the best products or better products than competitors unless we had irrefutable supporting evidence.

All communication, marketing and advertising materials had to be reviewed by Quality Assurance before use. We had to include our sources for facts and statistics cited in our materials.

Accordingly, I have little or no respect for people "who make it up as they go" and lie. I don't believe news I see on the internet unless it can be independently verified, such as through Snopes and Politifact.

~~~~~

In my time I've received a couple parking tickets and just one speeding ticket – in a school zone of all locations.

I was driving to work on a beautiful spring morning just before Easter. I usually traveled a residential street past the local middle school, then took a curvy road down the hill to town. For whatever reason, that morning I decided to take the more heavily monitored state route past the school.

Maybe I didn't see the school zone sign amid the fresh green foliage or just plain forgot about it amid the sunshine, but soon after I drove past the school, I looked in my rear-view mirror and was surprised to see a police cruiser with its lights flashing. I pulled off the road as soon as I was able, waited for the policeman, then accepted blame – and my ticket. If I recall correctly, I was driving at least 20 miles above the school zone limit, so it was a hefty fine.

I was mortified. At first, I was determined not to tell my parents. Then that evening, a family friend – among the dozens who had driven past me while I was stopped along the road – asked me what had happened. It was useless. If one person knew, then my parents were likely to find out. So I fessed up.

~~~~~

My mom always believed "Honesty is the best policy" – except in the weeks before Christmas when I believed in Santa Claus.

It's one of the great ironies of life.

Just when kids around the world are warned about the high behavioral standards set by a certain old man in red who's making a list and checking it twice, their parents are telling lots of lies, albeit as white as the new-fallen snow.

If your childhood was like mine, you were told that unless you behaved, Santa Claus wouldn't bring you any presents.

Ignore such warnings at your own peril, lest you find a chunk of Pennsylvania's best bituminous coal in your stocking Christmas morning.

You never suspected that it was all part of a ruse to make you behave for a month or two and thus save on your parent's supply of aspirin – including my parents' answers to questions from their trusting, gullible child concerning the personality of Santa Claus.

After one such conversation in our family living room, I believed that Santa possessed supernatural powers.

It was a late autumn evening, and I was lying on the living room floor, deeply engrossed in a new coloring book, while my mom watched TV and my dad read the newspaper.

What I did, or didn't do, that sparked the lecture which followed has long been forgotten. All I remember is that my mom told me that Santa knew what I was doing every second of the day.

I asked how that could be possible.

She said that Santa was in the room watching me that very minute. My eyes scanned the living room walls, ceiling and windows, but I couldn't see him. So, taking a page from my catechism, I asked if Santa was God.

My mom said no, but assured me that Santa knew when I was bad or good just the same.

Full of new respect for Santa, I returned to my coloring book and told myself that I had better watch out and better not cry.

Yep, Santa Claus was in the living room watching me alright. Little did I know, however, that "Santa" was relaxing on the couch reading our local newspaper.

I bought their bunk hook, line and sinker. No wonder I was upset every time I heard "I Saw Mommy Kissing Santa Claus." If I had to behave, then Santa should, too!

I finally learned the truth when I was 7, the evening after I overheard one of my classmates smugly informing another that there really wasn't a Tooth Fairy, so there was no reason to leave a lost tooth under a pillow.

I was shocked! My parents would never lie to me! Nevertheless, I promised myself to bring up the subject with my parents during supper that evening.

I told them what had happened at school, they fessed up about the Tooth Fairy.

They then asked if I had any other questions, say about Santa

Claus?

Talk about disillusionment! All my fantasies about the Tooth Fairy, Santa Claus and the Easter Bunny came crashing down in the same evening.

~~~~~

I recently told my mom that there have been a few times in my life that I've been tempted, sorely tempted, to do something that would have involved "living a lie." I added she was in my head each time, reminding me the importance of living an honest life.

You're not going to work in a sewing factory

Although I had three older female cousins, I was the first Lugar or Spampinato granddaughter to graduate from college.

Soon after I was born, a neighbor of my grandparents Spampinato told my mom that I would do well in school because of the shape of the back of my head; the lobe was rounded, not flat.

I attended kindergarten and first grade at our local public elementary school. During first grade, I was stricken with both measles and chicken pox. My mom was concerned that I had missed so much school that I would not advance to second grade. She talked with my teacher, who responded, "Oh, lost days won't keep Marianne back. She's a good student. She'll move on to second grade."

I did advance to second grade, but at our parish school, and remained in parochial school through high school. Because my mom didn't drive at the time, we didn't think there was a way for me to attend our parish school, as we lived on the other side of town. But then we learned about a special bus that transported students from outlying areas.

Grandma Lugar and me

Grandma Lugar, recalling how my mom struggled in school, remained concerned about my scholastic aptitude. She asked one of the nuns, who was related to us, how she thought I would do in school. Sister Magdalene replied, "Oh you don't have to worry about Marianne. She does fine."

When I was in middle school, another nun strongly encouraged my parents to send me to college and repeatedly told my mom that I was "college material."

I pulled mostly A's through K-8, high school and college and graduate school, with a few exceptions that I can recall. In addition to the "C" I received for my penmanship in third grade:

- High School Physics I and Algebra I: I still don't get physics, although I did well in chemistry, biology, geology and physiology. I don't think grade school prepared me well for high school math, although I did well after the first grading period.
- High School Gym: Remember, I'm a klutz. Girls' gym class was divided into segments – basketball, children's races and games, and square dancing. I kid you not. Four decades later, I still can't shoot hoops. I pulled a "B" only because we received extra points for taking our gym uniform home to be washed. I just about always wore a clean uniform.
- College Reporting I: Really. But then we learned that few students received higher than a "B" in the course. I pulled an "A" in Reporting II.
- Painting I: I could have taken a History of Art class for a humanities elective (and did so a couple of years later) but this bright-eyed and bushy tailed college freshman wanted to take a painting class. Our professor told us that if we completed our assignments on time, we would earn at least a "C." If we showed some talent, then our grade would be

The painting of Clark Gable, as seen in *Gone With the Wind,* that I painted in college.

higher. I must have shown some talent – perhaps with this painting – because I received a "B."

In high school, I was a National Merit Scholarship Semi-Finalist. I was accepted into the National Honor Society in my sophomore year, and amazingly, was also accepted into Mu Alpha Theta, the math honor society.

Meanwhile, my parents had experienced marital problems since I was in elementary school. I won't rehash the painful details except to note that my dad left home several times. They eventually reconciled each time, in part because my mom knew

My parents and me after my graduation from Duquesne University.

that his income – not to mention eliminating costs associated with a second household – would help toward parochial school tuition and my college education.

Just one example of the many sacrifices my mom made so I would receive a good education that would hopefully be followed by a successful professional career.

When I pursued my master's degree in Leadership and Liberal Studies, I was accepted into the American Red Cross continuing education program. It covered my tuition, while I paid for my books and transportation to Duquesne University.

~~~~~

Grandma Lugar could sew, knit and crochet. Mom took sewing classes when she was young and worked in a succession of sewing factories. She never knitted or crocheted. When I was a child, mom sewed many of my clothes. She fashioned clothes for my Barbie dolls. Once I started my career and bought my own clothes, mom hemmed my slacks. After she retired, our pastor recruited her to do some sewing and maintain the altar linens.

About all I can sew is a loose button. Mom recalls that the first time I sewed a button, onto my teddy bear, I couldn't even center the button.

Mom never pushed me to learn how to sew. Maybe she was afraid that I would settle for the work she did. More likely, she wanted me to identify and develop my own interests and talents.

And so I did. When I was in middle school, I wrote and designed my first holiday newsletter. I included scripture, holiday facts, trivia, crossword puzzles and other games. I continued this tradition for several years, also adding an Easter edition and a special "50" publication when mom hit that milestone age.

I was a teenager during the Watergate scandal. Impressed by the efforts of Woodward and Bernstein, I decided I wanted to pursue a career in Journalism. However, I soon realized that I lacked the temperament to become an investigative journalist.

When I was pursuing my bachelors in Journalism, I worked summers in the classified advertising department at our local daily newspaper. I'm sure that work experience helped a new college graduate land a job in her field a month after graduation.

The morning of my interview with the American Red Cross, mom left me a note, encouraging me to do my best and that if getting the job was God's will, nothing could stop me.

I had found life's work: communications, writing and public relations. No little thanks to my parents, especially my mom.

While I marvel at mom's ability to sew, she marvels at what I can do on the computer. We both know and accept that we each have skills that the other lacks.

I've been blessed to have a mom who expects me to live my own life – not hers.

Say please and thank you

The older I get, the more I see that what used to be considered common courtesy is no longer so common. And we're worse off for it.

I was taught that if you made a request of someone, you included the word "please." When someone helped you or did something nice for you, you must say "thank you."

When I received a gift for my birthday, Christmas, or another observance, my parents expected me to write thank you notes – and in a timely manner.

Common courtesy also included holding doors open for people; leaving a decent tip; giving a seat up for someone older than you; and returning shopping carts to the store or corral in the parking lot.

In addition to exchanging gifts within our department when I worked at the Red Cross, I bought snacks to be shared within support departments, such as IT, maintenance, receptionist (who often helped us with clerical tasks) and the office management group.

~~~~~

Since I'm a klutz, I've often said that I doubt I could ever be a waitress – at least not for more than a few days. I would likely spend most of my pay replacing broken dishes and meals I dropped on the floor.

That's why I tip at least 15 percent when I eat out. I want to recognize those who excel at what I would do poorly.

One year, our parish's pastoral minister invited me to assist with our church's annual "Celebration of Love," a special mass and dinner for married and engaged couples.

I had hoped I would be assigned to the kitchen to prepare the meal or wash dishes.

But no, I was asked to help serve the meal – salad and spaghetti. I distributed the salad plates easily enough. Then came the main course. Even though someone held the tray while I served the entrée, I was nervous. I took my time, careful not to spill any sauce.

My assigned table included several couples I was friends with. One of the husbands said, "Hey, hurry it up. I'm hungry."

I looked at him and replied, "I can take my time and not make a mess, or I can spill food over your lap. Which to you prefer?"

~~~~~

On a related note, I wish more people would follow the adage "If you can't say something nice, don't say anything" on social media. Even in retirement, I won't make time in my day to troll commenters and pages of entities I don't like. I'd rather read, walk my dog, paint, do a jigsaw puzzle…even watch paint dry.

Be humble

Hand in hand with being grateful is being humble.

One of my favorite sites among my travels is Saint Paul Cathedral in the City of London. It's where Prince Charles married Lady Diana Spencer, and where Diana's funeral was held 16 years later. It's the church in **Mary Poppins** where the "bird lady," played by actress Jane Darwell, sits on the steps and feeds the birds.

The current cathedral, the fourth church on the site located in the city's business center, survived the Luftwaffe's Blitz of London. Fire personnel spent night after night atop its roof to extinguish incendiary bombs that landed on the cathedral.

Behind the High Altar at the east end of the Cathedral is the American Memorial Chapel, also known as the Jesus Chapel. This part of the Cathedral was destroyed during the Blitz and as part of the restoration it was decided that the people of Britain should commemorate the 28,000 Americans stationed in the United Kingdom who lost their lives during World War II. The images that adorn its wood, metalwork and stained glass include depictions of the flora and fauna of North America (stpauls.co.uk).

Saint Paul Cathedral is also the final resting place of Sir Christopher Wren, the famous architect credited with rebuilding nearly 50 churches following the Great Fire of London in 1666 (which managed to have one good outcome – it killed the plague). The Cathedral is considered his masterpiece.

His memorial plaques in the floor and wall in a corner of the Cathedral crypt are simple compared to the majestic monuments to Lord Nelson and the Duke of Wellington located nearby.

Part of the stone's inscription, written in Latin: "Reader, if you seek his monument, look around you."

Our actions speak louder than words. What we do is more important than what we say we do. Talented, successful people don't have to tell us they are. We know, and we applaud.

~~~~~

My mom raised me to be humble. I wasn't to brag about my scholastic achievements or other accomplishments. I was gifted by God with certain talents and was to use these gifts to help others and to give glory to God.

As an adult, I received feedback from supervisors and others about my discomfort in receiving compliments. When someone complimented me, I seemed embarrassed and used to explain away or diminish my success. It took me some time to simply smile and say, "Thank you."

~~~~~

One of the joys of being semi-retired is being more available to help my mom with her shopping, errands and medical appointments. Actions speak louder than words, so such assistance is my putting my thanks into action.

Listen to your gut

My mom is a firm believer in women's intuition. She also likes to people watch. As a result, she's pretty accurate in reading people. She's read marital discord in a couple's physical distance.

One summer when I was in parochial school, we had to go to Pittsburgh to get my school uniforms because of some size issues. We were traveling on the Parkway East when my mom said, "What was that?" She heard a noise coming from the bottom of the car. My dad said the car was fine, but mom insisted that something was wrong. We exited the parkway and found that indeed something was very wrong with the car – the torsion bar suspension needed repair.

We managed to get the car to the first repair shop we found, and several hundred dollars later, were back on the road.

Everything comes in threes

My mom is less superstitious than me. She doesn't worry about black cats crossing her path or walking under a ladder. She doesn't toss spilled salt over her shoulder or knock twice on wood to prevent bad luck.

However, she does believe in itchy palms and that everything comes in threes.

When it comes to itchy palms, most believe that if your left hand itches, you're going to pay out money, and when your right hand itches, you're going to receive money. Mom may be right-handed, but she believes the opposite: you'll receive money when your left hand itches and have to spend it when your right hand itches.

For mom, "Everything comes in threes" is never about something good. The hot water tank goes kaput, followed by the washing machine – you worry and wait for what's going to break next.

Worse yet, two people we know die, and then she'd worry about who the third could be.

Take care of your teeth

Both my parents wore dentures; in my dad's case, partials. Perhaps because of the tough times during the Great Depression, mom's teeth were soft. She ended up wearing a full set of dentures.

Always wanting better for me, mom started taking me to the dentist when I was 4 or 5. If I had a good report, we would go to the flagship Penn Traffic department store, where she'd let me pick out a new Barbie outfit in the toy department.

We'd also have lunch in the Penn Traffic dining room. No matter how much mom suggested that I try something different, my order was the same: a hamburger with ketchup (Heinz 57, of course, we did live in western Pennsylvania) on the brioche-type rolls that Penn Traffic baked onsite, French fries and a fountain Coca-Cola.

After I lost my baby teeth, my permanent set of teeth came in crooked, and I had an overbite (from sucking my thumb? – mom may have thought so, but I don't remember her saying so). So much so than when I was in fifth grade, my parents agreed that I should be fitted for braces. I wore braces for two years, in sixth and seventh grade.

As if it wasn't bad enough that during my middle school years, I was overweight, wore thick glasses and started getting my period. Back then, braces weren't invisible, and I had to wear all-too-visible headgear for several hours each day to keep my teeth in alignment.

But thanks to my parents' tightening the purse strings, I entered high school with straight teeth. I can't imagine how self-conscious I would have been in my very public role as primary Red Cross spokesperson if I hadn't worn braces.

Take care of your back and stand up straight

For nearly as long as I can remember, my mom has suffered from bouts of intense back pain. Maybe her pain was from all those years sitting in front of a sewing machine working in a local garment factory. Maybe her bones, like her teeth, weren't as durable.

She's had a total of seven operations on her back, neck and knees.

Perhaps from years of carrying his mail bag on side (despite mom's encouragement to switch sites on occasion), dad also had back problems. In time, he had to give up carrying mail on a walking route and switch to a mounted route in a more rural part of town.

For years, mom has warned me to be careful carrying anything heavy. For example, my purse, which could possibly be considered a lethal weapon in many places.

My purse could rival Mary Poppins' magic bag as to what could be found in it. In addition to the usual wallet, hair brush, tissues, pens and phone, you'll find a toothbrush and toothpaste, grocery and other sale brochures, hand lotion, antibacterial gel, wet wipes, extra pads of checks, envelopes, stamps, address labels – and a crab pick.

~~~~~

In 2007, mom needed another operation but delayed in scheduling it because of my dad experiencing a deep low in his bipolar condition. Her surgeon insisted on the surgery, and, understanding how my dad's condition could impact her recovery, wanted her to spend several days in transitional care.

Realizing it time for me to reciprocate the care my parents gave me, I obtained permission to work from their home for about a month, as long as my parents installed an internet connection so I could carry out all of my responsibilities.

After the surgery, mom's iron levels were low, so much so that she needed blood transfusions, but didn't receive two units of red blood cells until she kept falling asleep during physical therapy. She was also on heavy pain medications.

One day when I visited her before the transfusions, she was depressed and fretting that she would never fully recover. She urged me to put her and my dad in a nursing home and sell their house.

I made a tactful retreat out the door, headed straight for the nurses' station and frantically asked, "What have you done with my mother? The woman in the room is not my mother. She's talking crazy. She's given up."

Mom finally received her transfusions a couple of days later and started to regain her strength and focus. She may not have been "as good as new," but she did stop talking about going to a nursing home.

Under, not over

Look in the two bathrooms in my house and you might be surprised to see that the toilet paper rolls are installed so that the paper falls under (beneath the roll), not over (on top of the roll).

No matter that the patent for the toilet paper holder shows paper flowing "over" the roll, nor that two-thirds of the United States population votes "over." (businessinsider.com/patent-shows-right-way-to-hang-toilet-paper-2015-3)

Mom influenced me to go "under" so that the paper doesn't stick out from the wall. This method also may prevent the user from unrolling too much paper, which was a major consideration in my parents' house.

My dad never understood why my mom and I used more toilet paper than he did.

"I hear you up in the bathroom," he'd say. "Brrmm, brrmm, brrmm goes the holder. You use too much toilet paper!"

Plain black (coffee)

My mom and James Bond are as different as night and day, but both have beverage orders synonymous with them.

For my mom, it's coffee, plain black.

Among the many sacrifices my mom has made over the years is abstaining from coffee while she was pregnant with me. She couldn't stand the taste of it during her pregnancy. One of her first requests after giving birth?

Coffee, plain black.

Blame her aversion to coffee during her pregnancy on me. I can't stand the taste of the stuff. I've never had a cup of coffee (on purpose - on occasion, my order of black tea has been mistakenly filled as black coffee).

Although my lineage does not include the British Isles, you'd never know it from my choice of morning beverage. Black tea, no cream, one Splenda.

SHORT TAKES
The fruit doesn't fall far from the tree

My mom has long believed that parents are the first – and best – examples for their children. If parents attend church with their children on a regular basis, their children will be more likely to be regular churchgoers.

If parents don't smoke, their children are less likely to smoke. Parents who swear and use foul language shouldn't be surprised when their children do the same (cue "F-U-D-G-E" in *A Christmas Story*).

If kids catch their parents in a lie, trust can be lost.

~~~~~

It could always be worse

When some say, "look on the bright side," my mom prefers, "It could always be worse."

Have an infestation of flesh flies in your basement (as I had one summer)? It could always be worse – they could be in your bedroom, bathroom or kitchen.

In an automobile accident? Are you OK if your car isn't? See, it could always be worse. Better to repair a car than lose your life.

~~~~~

Watch where you're going and look both ways before you cross the street

This mom saying is so ingrained in my that I look both ways once, twice, three times before crossing a street when I walk or drive.

Good thing, since multiple vehicles, including two school buses, have turned left in front of me when I had the green light to go straight. It was too dark to catch the number of the first school bus, but you better believe I caught and reported the number of the school bus the second time this happened.

Galla, my rescue dog, is intelligent but seems oblivious when it comes to watching for traffic. Sometimes, drivers stop at intersections on side streets will motion us to cross, but I respond, "Thanks, but my dog has to learn to watch for traffic when we cross the street."

~~~~~

Be careful what you wish for…you might get it

My mom has fantasized about winning the Powerball for years. Ever since I saw the movie **Waking Ned Devine,** I've told her that if she indeed hit "the big one," she would have a major heart attack, collapse and die.

As I review my life, there have been many times when I wanted something desperately, such as a promotion at work, and have been disappointed not to receive what I wanted. Then as time passed, I realize whatever I wanted wasn't all what it was cracked up to be.

A Mother's Faith and Love

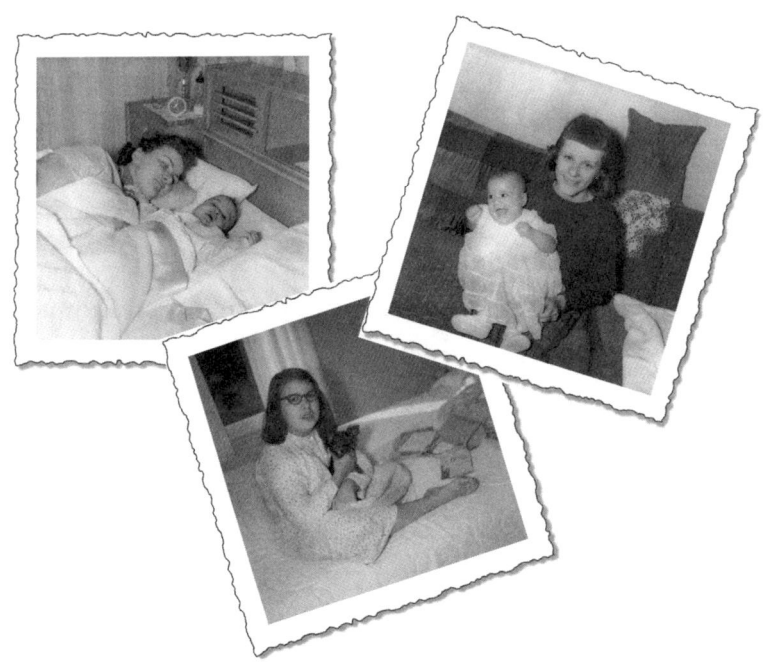

God writes straight with crooked lines

My mom left high school after 10th grade to work in a local sewing factory, but stopped working after she and my dad married in 1957. After he graduated high school in 1950, my dad worked at Bethlehem Steel and served in the United States Navy for a total of four years.

The United Steelworkers of America called a work stoppage against Bethlehem Steel when my parents were expecting me. Times were tough; they lived mostly on savings. My dad had caddied at a local country club when he was a kid, but since many Bethlehem Steel managers were members of the club, striking workers were often passed over as caddies.

The year after I was born, my dad was laid off. Mom got a job at the Penn Traffic department store in downtown Johnstown to make ends meet; she was hired to work in linens, but was moved to the toy department. Her supervisors liked her as an employee, but when my dad was called back to work, she left her position to resume life as a full-time mom.

One of our neighbors was a letter carrier. He suggested that my dad take the civil service exam to seek employment as a letter carrier. He added that dad's naval service would be factored into the application process. My dad was hired to run evening collections. He'd exit the mill and walk over to the post office. He eventually quit the mill, taking a pay cut to obtain full-time employment at the post office.

The car we had in 1968 required major repairs, for which my parents arranged payments. I was in third grade when my mom decided she should return to work to help with household costs.

It was a tough transition for her as she had not worked full-time in 11 years.

When our furnace had to be replaced the following month,

mom made up her mind that she had to continue working, no matter how difficult it was to return to the routine.

She stuck it out, working in two undergarment manufacturers and one shoe factory, until she retired at age 63. She received higher Social Security payments than my dad, who earned a civil service pension while working at the post office. She continues to save money every month.

You never know what you can do until you try

One of the best things my dad ever did was encourage, that is, urge, mom to learn how to drive.

His most unusual accomplishment may have been teaching three generations of Lugar women how to drive. He taught my Grandma Lugar, my mom, and me.

Mom obtained her license at age 42. She seldom drove far, except to give my dad a brief break when we went on vacation.

During the last four years of his life, my dad was unable to drive because of having been diagnosed with a mild case of Parkinson's disease, as well as because of other medications he had taken. Although my mom doesn't drive in wintry weather, she was able to get him to most of their medical appointments because he taught her how to drive four decades earlier.

~~~~~

Most of my friends have a hard time believing that I'm an introvert, even when I noted that every Myers-Briggs test I've taken has the same result: ISFJ – Introverted Sensing with Extroverted Feeling.

Mom recalls me being a shy child, a child who wasn't talkative. Occasionally when she saw me lector at Sunday Mass or caught a television interview of me, she would comment, "Who would have thought that a child who seldom opened her mouth would talk so much today?"

When it came to work, I did what was expected of me in my position. However, I hated watching news clips of myself. I always found fault with my "ums" and "ers," as well as my frequent blinking, particularly when I wore contacts. I found I could maintain eye contact better wearing glasses, perhaps there

> Yes, I've kissed the Blarney Stone, but I still would rather be the interviewer than the interviewee, in the audience instead of speaking.

was a more noticeable physical barrier between me and the outside world.

Becoming more involved in my home parish, which was merged in 2009, in my mid-twenties resulted in making new friends, friends who genuinely cared for and supported each other. I have served on numerous boards and committees, but such service never helped my self-confidence as much as my full participation in the former Saint Rochus Parish.

~~~~~

When I was a kid, in the evenings my dad would often open a world map and lay it on the floor. He would point out countries and directions.

My mom recalls one time when she was baking bread, I kept pestering her about what she was doing. I asked her about each ingredient, and, when it came to yeast, I replied, "Are you also going to put in some west, north and south?"

We didn't have **Sesame Street** in my formative years. Instead, we had **Captain Kangaroo.** Each episode included a travelogue, a film of some distant locale, with a version of "Far Away Places (with those strange-sounding names)" as background music.

I loved that segment. I was hooked. I longed to be old enough to travel the world. When I got a summer job in the classified ads department at our local daily newspaper after I graduated high school (returning to the job the next three summer vacations from college), I spent some earnings on clothes (after all, I had worn a parochial school uniform for the past 11 years) and saved the rest for a trip to Europe.

Mom, who at this point hadn't flown on an airplane, was worried sick. What if the airplane went down in the ocean, and she would never see me again? Believe me, over the years she's worried more about that than bedbugs.

I settled on taking a trip through the American Institute for Foreign Study. It was akin to the tour taken in the movie **If it's Tuesday, it Must be Belgium:** fly to London, spend two days there, then take the ferry from Dover to Ostend, Belgium, then onto a day in Amsterdam, two days in Paris, followed by a day in Geneva, concluding with a day in Florence and two days in Rome, then fly home. Whew.

What can I say? I was 19 and wanted to experience a bit of several countries, hoping to return to my favorites for further exploration in the future.

My parents took me to the Greater Pittsburgh International Airport to catch my flight to New York. Having never been on an airplane before, I was petrified. I was fortunate to be seated next to an older lady, a veteran traveler, who coached me through my first flight.

The trip, although hectic, was awesome. We stayed in college dorms in London and Switzerland, low-cost hotels in Paris and Italy, and in the Netherlands, we roomed with private citizens. The fact that I've returned to Great Britain three times and to France twice should tell you that London and Paris were my favorites.

Although my perspective may have been shaded by the fact that by the time we reached Rome, I had come down with a cold – and had my period.

AIFS uses charter flights, and the plane we took out of Rome had to refuel at Shannon International Airport in Ireland, where a maintenance issue was discovered.

We finally arrived at JFK International in New York City hours after our scheduled arrival time. I had missed my flight to Pittsburgh, where my parents were already waiting for me.

The charter airline tried to get me on the next U.S. Airways flight (yes, this was a long time ago) to Pittsburgh, but I was placed on standby. My checked luggage went on without me. At this point, I somehow reached my parents and begged them to come get me, a delusional thought I now chalk up to my fatigue, my cold – and hormones.

I learned that the U.S. Airways terminal was a short walk from the terminal for the charter airline. Hand luggage in hand, I stormed over to U.S. Airways and insisted I be put on the next flight to Pittsburgh. The ticket counter staff checked and told me the next flight was out of LaGuardia Airport early in the morning. They booked me, and even gave me $10 cab fare to get me to LaGuardia (I told you this was a LONG time ago).

It's about midnight, and I'm by myself in a cab (another first) with a driver for whom English is a second language. If my mom had known, she probably would have taken a heart attack.

The cab driver may not have spoken the best English, but

when we arrived and found what appeared to be deserted terminal, he waited to make sure I could enter, which I was able to do. As I familiarized myself with my new surroundings, I found groups of fellow travelers from the AIFS trip around every corner.

That night, while my parents slept in a terminal at Greater Pittsburgh International Airport, I was too worked up to sleep. Besides, I wanted to keep an eye on my hand luggage.

When my parents and I finally returned home, I took a bath and slept into the next day. At one point, I was in such a deep sleep my mom thought I had died.

In less than two weeks, I went from a weak-kneed, nervous first-time traveler to holding my own with airline ticket counter staff.

Grandma Lugar, who, at age 17 crossed an ocean traveling by herself on an ocean liner, would be proud.

~~~~~

In my mid-30s, I decided to pursue a graduate degree. I researched several programs, then settled on Duquesne University's Masters in Leadership and Liberal Studies program. I often referred to the program being an MBA for a right-brained person.

I completed the program over four years instead of the usual two; it was challenging enough to maintain my workload and community commitments by taking one course each semester, let alone two. I watched little or no television, even on Sundays, devoting that time to completing my required reading.

Looking back on this time, I don't know how I did it. But I did, earning A's in every course.

Walk with God: When God closes a door, He opens a window

Sometimes when mom says this, I respond, "So we can jump out the window."

I'm sure I'm not alone in experiencing several disappointments during my life. Yet people have noted my resilience in overcoming loss and moving on.

Shortly after my cancer diagnosis, I was discussing my experience with a breast cancer survivor. She was surprised to hear me say how lucky I had been. I replied that for my ovarian cancer to be diagnosed early, I was indeed lucky. Most of the women I took chemotherapy with had more advanced cancers, diagnosed in Stage III or IV. I've often wondered how many of them are still alive. Here I am enjoying my semi-retirement, with time to help my mom and relax on my couch with my rescue dog. I am indeed lucky.

~~~~~

When people ask me how I could retire at 55, I reply, "It's amazing how much money you can save when you don't marry and don't have children."

I used to feel inadequate not having a husband or children, then I realize that I never felt "compelled" to have either. I continually try to accept God's will for my life, and that if I was to be married, I would have consciously made it happen.

We pray in our time, but God answers in His time

One of the greatest mysteries in my life is why my Cousin Suzie was killed in a car accident just weeks after beginning her freshman year at the University of Pittsburgh. At the time, our local Pitt campus didn't have a four-year nursing program, so Suzie had enrolled at the Oakland main campus.

She was traveling with two other students from Ebensburg and one of their parents who had driven to Pittsburgh to bring them home for the weekend. When a tractor trailer struck the rear driver's side of their car, my cousin was killed instantly. Everyone else in the car, as well as the truck driver, walked away from the accident.

My Aunt Donna and Uncle Fred were devastated. Suzie was a great kid and did well in school. She enjoyed reading, skiing, music and team sports, and made friends quickly. As my aunt often recalled, my cousin never gave her any heartache while she was alive, but so many tears followed after her death.

The Ebensburg community came out in droves to comfort them and pay their respects to my cousin. For many years, I often joined my parents in visiting with my aunt and uncle on the

Aunt Donna, my godmother, holding me when I was an infant.

weekends.

Aunt Donna, who was born when my mom was age 13, was the only one of six siblings to take after the petite Mateljan side of the family instead of the stockier Lugar side. She and my mom were extremely close, so close that mom chose her to be my godmother.

Aunt Donna was the first Lugar sibling to die. She passed away from cancer complications at age 54, two years to the day she was diagnosed.

I doubt I'll ever forget that Thanksgiving Day when Aunt Donna died. Because of my aunt's condition, mom didn't thaw a turkey or prepare a large meal. Instead she made breaded pork chops, one of Uncle Fred's favorite meals, and persuaded him to leave my aunt's bedside long enough to eat with us.

Mom had visited that morning, and dad and I were going to join her in returning to the hospital after we washed dishes. *It's a Wonderful Life* was on television. At the end of the movie, just as Zuzu says, "Look, daddy. Teacher says every time a bell rings, an angel gets his wings," the telephone rang.

Aunt Donna and me after my high school graduation. She also witnessed my graduation from Pitt-Johnstown, but died while I was attending graduate school.

It was another aunt calling to let us know that my Aunt Donna had just died. I've shared this experience with others, and, like me, they've gotten chills just hearing about it.

My Uncle Fred died unexpectedly from a heart attack in 2005. Unbeknownst to me or my parents, he and my aunt had named me executrix of their estate and co-residual heir.

Not a day goes by that I don't think of them and wonder what could have been. I would gladly return what they've given to me to have them back, for them to have the chance to see my Cousin Suzie graduate college, marry and have their grandchildren.

Only God knows why…

Let me kiss it and make it better

I always remember my mom being there for me, no matter what. Since my mom was more of a disciplinarian than my dad, I was a daddy's girl when I was young. That changed after my parents' marriage woes worsened. She was always there for me. I increasingly saw my mom as my defender and protector.

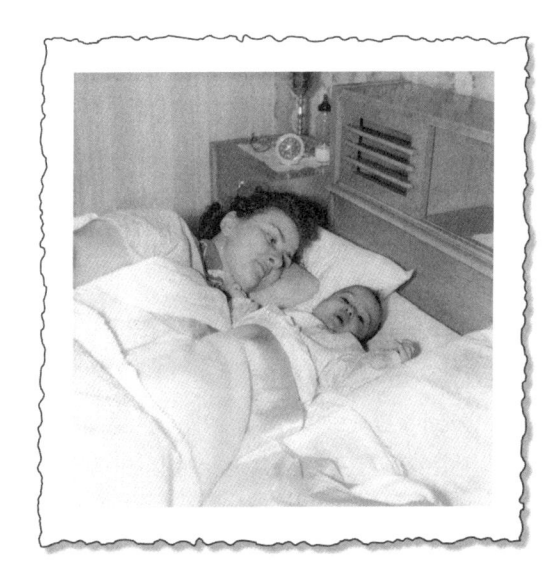

Mom and me in bed when I was an infant.

~~~~~

When I was in elementary school, school buses did not stop in front of your house. I had to walk two blocks down our alley to the bus stop, which was designated along a well-traveled street.

My walk to the bus stop took me past a German Shepherd dog that was kept on a short leash in a back yard along my route. The dog barked ferociously every time anyone walked past it. My mom had returned to work by this time, and when she and a neighbor walked to the bus stop to take a bus to the sewing factory, she often commented, "When that dog barks, it feels like it's climbing up my back."

I knew better than to go anywhere near that dog. One year, on our last school day before Easter (parochial school kids always had off on Holy Thursday and Good Friday), we made little candy baskets out of cottage cheese containers.

That afternoon, as I carried my candy basket up the alley, the dog broke loose from its chain and came after me. It pushed me to the ground. Fortunately, my dad was off that day, and had already come to the end of our yard to welcome me home from school.

He rushed down the alley, picked up the dog and threw it off me. He picked me up and got me into our car and started off for the hospital emergency room. Mom and our neighbor were walking up the road from their bus and she frantically asked, "What happened?"

The dog was taken away.

At the hospital, we saw that the dog had bitten my leg and scratched my back through my school uniform, although my clothing was not torn. I received one stitch to close the bite wound.

For months after this incident, I was afraid of dogs – any dogs, even my Grandma Lugar's old, overweight chihuahua named Chiquita.

Me holding Mitzi shortly after we got her.

We had a parakeet at the time, and one day when my parents and I went to the pet store for bird food, mom looked around while dad and I picked up and paid for the bird food.

When we returned home, mom kept talking about a pretty little dog she saw there, a dog that kept looking at her. We had no idea what she was talking about, so returned to the store to look at the long-haired chihuahua. This was shortly after Christmas, and the gentle dog was leftover inventory.

We bought her and named her Sweet Mitzi Peanuts. Not only did she help me get over my fear of dogs, she helped me get through my teenage years. In return, when Mitzi needed digitalis and other medicines as she aged, I was the only one who could get her to take her pills. Mitzi died in our arms a year or two after I started working at the Red Cross.

My mom wasn't there when I was hurt, but she knew what I needed to heal.

~~~~~

A weird thing happened as I was writing this book, which was nearly 50 years after I was bitten by the dog. I guess I bumped the area of my right leg where the dog bit me. The area had been barely discernible for years, but it was bruised after I hit my leg in that area. The stitched area must have opened or rose to the surface, because small scabs appeared at the stitch marks, and I was able to pull out a quarter-inch piece of thread.

I took it as evidence that no matter how hard we try, the effects of some wounds – be they physical, psychological or emotional – don't completely heal, and we can't be sure that effects won't resurface someday.

~~~~~

One holiday season, my parents quarreled, and my dad decided to spend Christmas with his family instead of with my mom and me. I was heartbroken. My mom and I went to morning Mass, then we went over to my Grandparents Lugars' home.

Years later, my mom told me what my Aunt Donna told her that day. She told my mom that she wanted to hug me tight, but was afraid that I was so fragile that I would break.

~~~~~

About halfway through writing this book, mom reminded me of our "bathroom talks," which occurred when I needed to discuss something important, well, at least important to me. At these times, either mom or I were taking our bath while the other sat on the toilet, which faced the bathtub.

She consoled me outside of the bathroom as well, including when the boy I liked didn't ask me to my senior prom.

My parents remodeled the bathroom when I was in college. The bathtub was surrounded by three walls, blocking the view of someone seated on the toilet, newly positioned along the short wall encasing the tub.

After a while, I told my mom that the new bathroom layout made me feel as though I was in a confessional instead of a bathroom, so we found another way to talk.

~~~~~

When I was in my mid-30s, I began experiencing irregular menstrual cycles. I had light bleeding one month, then heavy bleeding the next, accompanied by painful cramping. My periods often came sooner than or later than 28 days. I was often moody or overly emotional before and during my period, and this was beginning to affect my effectiveness at work.

The male gynecologist I had at the time told me I was nearing menopause, so nothing to worry about. I wasn't happy with his answer or his apparent disinterest, so didn't have an exam for a couple of years.

When I neared 40, I decided that I needed to resume getting annual gynecological exams. However, instead of making an appointment with my usual physician, I instead selected a female nurse practitioner.

She confirmed that what I was experiencing was not normal for someone my age. She encouraged me to chart my cycles and eventually put me on a low-dose birth control pill to try to regulate my cycles. When that didn't work, I underwent a uterine biopsy, which proved to be benign.

At the time, I had my pap smear each October, which is my birth month. After my exam in 2000, I was notified that although my results were normal, an insufficient sample had been taken, so I should return for another test, which would be covered by insurance, in six months.

Perplexed that my cycles continued to be irregular, the nurse practitioner scheduled me to undergo a uterine ultrasound. After the procedure was completed, I waited and waited. I knew something was wrong.

After what seemed to be hours, the nurse practitioner told me that the ultrasound showed that I had severe endometriosis. Plus, there seemed to be a shadow on my left ovary. I felt sick and wanted to run away. But I couldn't leave until I was scheduled to undergo a hysterectomy and gave a blood sample for a CA-125 test.

At this time, I had not yet informed my parents of the extent of difficulties I had been experiencing. I broke down, called them, and went to their house to tell them what was happening.

A few days later, I was contacted to meet with the surgeon I had selected to perform the operation. He explained that my CA-125 count, which should be less than 35, was more than 300. He strongly encouraged me to see a gynecological oncologist at UPMC Magee Medical Center.

I was shaken. Trying to talk myself and the surgeon out of being concerned, I replied that I had done some reading, and learned that the CA-125 results were not necessarily predictive of cancer. An acquaintance had told me that her mother had been diagnosed with ovarian cancer, but her CA-125 test was normal. The acquaintance's CA-125 results were high, but when she underwent her hysterectomy, only endometriosis was found.

The physician said that while the test is imprecise, if I had my surgery in Johnstown, no surgeon in the practice was board-approved to take lymph nodes for screening if indeed cancer was found.

So I made an appointment for UPMC. My parents accompanied me, and after meeting with the surgeon there, scheduled my hysterectomy for late afternoon on a Friday.

As I was coming out of the anesthesia after my surgery, I saw my mom standing over me. I asked her what had happened.

She told me what the surgeon instructed her to say – that they found cancer. I replied, "I have cancer."

Mom said, "No, you had cancer. They found it and removed it."

My surgeon wasn't on call over the weekend, but I was seen by residents and interns, but no one told me much more than my mom had.

Monday morning, my surgeon came to my room and said, "You don't know how fortunate you are. When we removed your reproductive organs, I thought it was a simple hysterectomy. When they came back and said they found two grape-sized tumors in your left ovary, I almost fell over. We don't find this cancer that early."

No cancer cells were found in my lymph nodes, so my cancer was diagnosed as being Stage I, but because the tumor cells were Grade B, my surgeon recommended three chemotherapy treatments, which turned into six treatments.

I remained in the hospital for a total of five days and nights. We spent both my dad's birthday and Mother's Day at the hospital. Every night except the last one, mom slept in a chair beside my bed in my room. On the fifth night, I told her I was OK, and that she should sleep in the room in an unused portion of the hospital that family members could rent for a few dollars a night.

I was violently ill for several days after my return home. I couldn't keep any food down. I recuperated at my house because my bedroom, bathroom, living room and kitchen were on the main floor.

When my Uncle Fred, about ready to return to Ebensburg from his winter home in Florida, called me, we both cried as I told him that "Aunt Donna was looking out for me. She had to be."

Mom stayed with me for at least four weeks, through trying on a wig and my first chemotherapy treatment, which was immediately followed by excruciating pain.

Mom was always there for me when I needed her the most. And no matter what the future brings, her wit and wisdom will be a part of me.

Acknowledgements

This book may not have been written if not for my experience writing for **Our Town,** published by Schurz Communications. Thank you to Brian Whipkey, editor, **The Daily American,** and Bruce Siwy, editor, **Our Town,** for welcoming me as a freelance correspondent and columnist, starting the week after I retired from the American Red Cross. Thanks also to Tom Koppenhofer, advertising director, and Mindy Faidley, graphic designer, for their publishing expertise.

I'm grateful to fellow freelance writer and editor Beth Ann Lombardi for reviewing an early draft and providing feedback – and catching errors that are difficult for authors to notice in their own work.

I first met graphic designer Joanne Mekis more than two decades ago while volunteering for our former Saint Rochus Parish, and have long admired her artistic skills. As we've shared stories of our childhood over the years (including that we both made our own Barbie doll furniture – I made mine using the removable plastic lids from aerosol cans and wire hangers bent to make the back of a chair), I knew she was the ideal illustrator for **Listen to Your Mother.**

Thank you, Holly Lees, for your creativity in photographing mom and me for this book. We've seldom looked as good!

I'm grateful to family and friends for their feedback and support; to media outlets that have increased awareness of this book; and to local organizations that have held book signings and are displaying my book.

Last, but most importantly, thanks to my mom, Betty Lugar Spampinato. Her love and support made this book – not to mention my life – possible. Thank you, mom.